Underwater Guide to the
RED SEA

Underwater Guide to the
RED SEA

Lawson Wood

JOHN BEAUFOY PUBLISHING

This edition published in the United Kingdom in 2023 by John Beaufoy Publishing Limited,
11 Blenheim Court, 316 Woodstock Road, Oxford OX2 7NS, U.K.
www.johnbeaufoy.com

10 9 8 7 6 5 4 3 2 1

Great care has been taken to maintain the accuracy of the information contained in this work. However,
neither the publishers nor the author can be held responsible for any consequences arising from the use
of the information contained therein.

ISBN 978-1-913679-36-1

Designed by Gulmohur Press
Project management by Rosemary Wilkinson

Printed and bound in Malaysia by Times Offset (M) Sdn. Bhd.

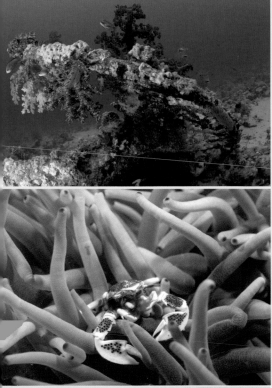

Contents

6 **Introduction to the Red Sea**
8 Geography
9 Geology
10 History
12 Climate
14 Practicalities

16 **The Marine Environment**
18 Open Ocean
18 Reef Structures
22 Life on the Coral Reef
24 Reef Relationships
29 Threats
30 Marine Conservation

32 **Diving and Snorkelling in the Red Sea**
34 Health and Safety
37 Equipment
38 Underwater Photography
41 Certification and Experience
42 Diving Facilities

44 **Guide to Dive Sites**
74 **Guide to Snorkel Spots**
86 **Marine Creature Identification**
153 **Glossary**
154 **Useful Contacts and Further Reading**
155 **Acknowledgements**
156 **Index**

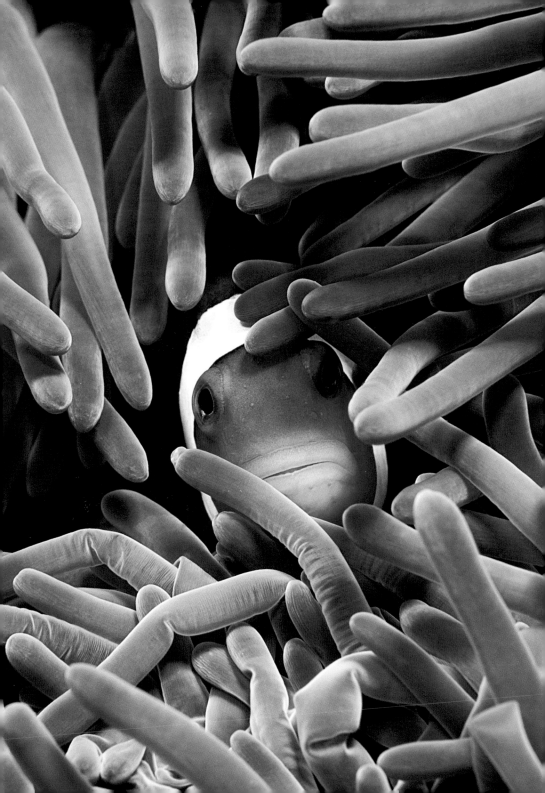

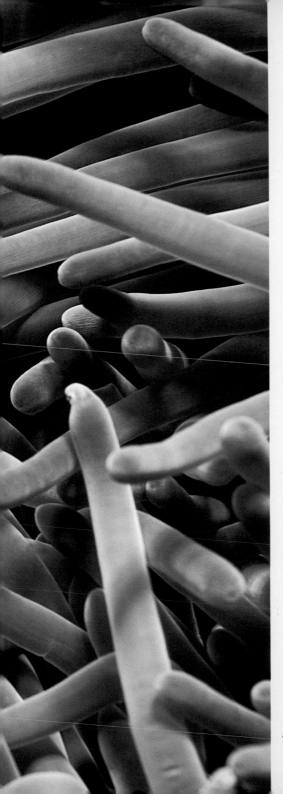

Introduction to the Red Sea

The brilliant soft coral gardens and millions of anthias are synonymous with the perception of the Red Sea with its vertical walls, fabulous shipwrecks and coral canyons. Diving is always excellent all year round here, but during the summer months of July through to September huge concentrations of fish congregate off the walls. There are a large number of endemic species peculiar to the Red Sea; however you should also expect to see the very best of what the entire Indian Ocean has to offer.

Anemones and clownfish are favourites of all the species in the Red Sea.

Geography

With a surface area of around 438,000 km² (169,100 sq. miles), the Red Sea is described as a Global 200 ecoregion, listed by the World Wide Fund for Nature (WWF) as a priority for conservation due to its exceptional biodiversity. It is bordered to the east by Jordan and Saudi Arabia, to the north by Israel and Egypt, to the west by Egypt, Sudan and Yemen and to the south by Djibouti, Eritrea and Somalia.

The Red Sea is an extension of the Great Rift Valley and separates the African continent from the Middle East and Asia. It extends from the Straits of Hormuz in the south to the massive, V-shaped Sinai Peninsula, where the Red Sea splits in two with the shallower, western arm stretching up towards the Mediterranean through the Gulf of Suez. The eastern arm, the Gulf of Aqaba, is a continuation of the Great Rift Valley, which extends up through Israel at Eilat.

The Red Sea is the most northerly tropical coral reef to Europe and a direct offshoot of the Indian Ocean. At over 2,250 km (1,400 miles) long, its widest part is opposite Massawa in Eritrea where it is 355 km (220 miles) across. At its southern end, it feeds through the 26-km (16-mile) wide pass at the Bab el-Mandeb Strait into the Indian Ocean. The main delight for scuba divers is the fact that over 40 per cent of the Red Sea is under 100 m (330 ft), making much of the region completely accessible to most divers; the deeper reefs are perfect for exploration by technical divers. The deepest part of the Red Sea is a narrow trough over 2,500 m (8,200 ft) deep and this feeds much of the region with cold upwellings, which combine with the more

The Sinai Peninsula is home to some of the best diving in the Red Sea.

Ras Muhammed sits at the apex of the Red Sea, the Gulf of Suez and the Gulf of Aqaba.

temperate coastal zone creating tremendous planktonic movements that fuel and replenish the reefs.

Geology

Around five million years ago the northern part of the Red Sea was connected to the Mediterranean, but as the land gradually uplifted, the Mediterranean connection closed as the Nile delta continued to expand. Subsequently the Red Sea basin became a gigantic evaporation plain with a few active volcanoes erupting through the rift. These huge layers of salt would ultimately keep the salinity level of the Red Sea much higher than any other sea. A couple of million years later, the Strait of Perim in the south opened. (Perim is now a volcanic island in the Strait of Mandeb that splits the Strait into two channels.) This resulted in the Red Sea now becoming an annex of the Indian Ocean and the in-rush of tropical waters brought all of the associated species of fish and invertebrate that we still enjoy today, although some species have now migrated into the Gulf

of Oman and even the eastern Mediterranean through the Suez Canal.

Come forward somewhat to around 15,000 years ago to the last Ice Age when so much water was locked in the polar caps, and once more the Red Sea became isolated from the Indian Ocean. This triggered the evolutionary processes that eventually resulted in the high numbers of endemic species.

Dive boats drop divers off underneath the headland.

History

The Red Sea was originally called the Arabian Gulf or Sea of Erythrias and there are several theories as to the origins of the name, including the colour of the beautiful red soft corals *Dendronephthya klunzingeri* and *D. hemprichi*; the periodic red tide produced by the bacteria *Trichodesmium erythraeum* and the *Sea of Reeds* dating back to the Biblical story of the Exodus. Some suggest it is because of the mineral-rich red mountains nearby called Harei Edom. Edom (סודא ירה) also means 'ruddy complexion' and is another name for Esau, the red-faced brother of Jacob, whose nation is descended from him. It may even be from the local Himyarites whose name means 'red'. One final theory in the mix states that the ancient Egyptians called their land *Dashret* or 'Red Land' and the sea became known as the 'Sea of the Red Land'. Take your pick!

One very early mention of the Red Sea is from 3,500 BC, when an expedition was sent down the sea to the ancient land of Punt. There were written references to Punt over a 2,000-year period but to this day no scholars have actually found the fabled land. Of course, we all know the story of Moses and the Israelites crossing the Red Sea (*Yam Suph*) to escape slavery in Egypt that is told in the Old Testament, Exodus 13:17 — 15:21.

When the Roman emperor, Augustus (27 BC–AD 14) controlled all of the Mediterranean and the northern Red Sea, it was the favoured route for the Romans to forge their trade links with India. Chinese goods were then introduced to the Romans via these Indian ports. During Medieval times, the importance of these trade routes for spices continued and when Napoleon Bonaparte invaded Egypt in 1798, he saw the advantage of expanding the existing canal system between the Red Sea and the Mediterranean. However, his vision failed due to incorrect calculations of

Black-breasted Pipefish live amongst soft corals.

Colourful soft corals are synonymous with the Red Sea.

the difference between the water levels of the Mediterranean and Red Seas leading to the belief that the disparity between them was too great. Eventually the French joined up with the Egyptians to form the Universal Company of the Maritime Suez Canal. Completion of the work took ten, problem-filled years. The canal was opened on 17 November 1869 changing the future of the Red Sea more than any other man-made construction.

The Suez Canal

The completion of the Suez Canal was the final stage of the very early canal works, first started during the reigns of the Pharaohs. Sesostris or the Pharaoh Senustret III of the Twelfth Dynasty (1897–1839 BC) is said to have started the first canal, but this was abandoned when he discovered that the sea level was higher than the Nile. The Persian King, Darius I had the same idea and managed to connect Lake Timsah with the Great Bitter Lake. Ptolemy II extended this by excavating a trench 30 m (100 ft) wide by 9 m (30 ft) deep and connected the lakes further. The Punt expedition under Hatshepsut was said to have finally connected the Red Sea with the Nile Delta (and thence the Mediterranean) by the 13th century BC.

The next modern attempt was undertaken by Napoleon Bonaparte who thought that by building the canal, he would either force the British to pay dues to France or force them to travel the great distances around South Africa. Sadly his engineers' calculations were wrong and again work was abandoned. It wasn't until the mid-1800's that the project got underway when Ferdinand de Lesseps convinced the Egyptian viceroy Said Pasha to support it. The Suez Canal (as we know it today) now connects Port Said in the Red Sea to Alexandria on the Mediterranean and is 193.30 km (120 miles) long. It was officially opened on 7 November 1869. After the closure of the canal from 1967 to 1975 because of the Six-Day War, it never regained its trading supremacy and many companies still prefer the old Cape route as it is much more politically stable.

Climate

The predominant climatic changes in the Red Sea region are a direct result of two distinct monsoon seasons in the summer and winter months bringing wind and rain. These monsoon winds are caused by the differential heat exchange between the sea and the land surface. The northern Red Sea is dominated by persistent winds from the north-west, but they rarely rise above 12 kmh (7 mph). Other wind patterns are very variable and seasonally reversible. The Egyptian Red Sea is perfect for diving all year round and indeed, I have lived in the country over extended periods of time and it was only on very rare occasions that I was unable to get in the water.

Temperatures on land can reach a high of 40°C (104°F) in August and fall to 20°C (68°F) in the winter (December to February), but you must remember that this is a very dry atmosphere with virtually zero humidity, so hydration is essential, as sweat quickly wicks from your skin. Rainfall is very scarce, with only around 60 mm (2⅓ in) per year, which usually only falls in the coastal zone in short bursts associated with a thunderstorm. Dust storms are frequent.

Sea temperature and visibility

For the most part the Red Sea is incredibly clear because there are no large river run-offs and the deep water catches any detritus, leaving the shallow diving waters unclouded. During the summer months, the very high surface temperatures combined with the scarcity of rainfall and the fact that there is no major supply of fresh water to the Red Sea result in very high evaporation levels, which can be as much as 205 cm (81 in) per year, and high salinity, making this one of the hottest and saltiest seas in the world with minimal seasonal variation.

The average temperature during the summer is about 26°C (79°F) in the north and 30°C (86°F) in the south, with only about 2°C (3.6°F) variation during the winter months, but it can fall to a cooler 21°C (70°F) in February.

The wind is the driving force of the Red Sea and will transport planktonic material either in suspension or as bedload, making the currents essential for their role in the erosion of coastal rock and feeding submerged coral reefs. Visibility is therefore generally very good all year round particularly off the main vertical walls, such as the Straits of Tiran and Ras Muhammad in the north and the Brothers, Elphinstone and Daedalus in the south. Shallower reefs may be affected by windy conditions which stir up the sandy shallows, however overall the visibility is rarely below 18 m (60 ft) and is more often well in excess of 45 m (50 ft).

The Red Sea is diveable all year round.

Anthias are the most common of all the Red Sea reef fish.

Practicalities

Millions of dollars have been spent on the tourism infrastructure not only on roads, airports and communications, but also on reclaiming what is in fact a very arid, inhospitable terrain on the shores of the Red Sea. Marinas, beach development and watersports have all had an enormous impact on the shoreline communities of the Red Sea, though not always beneficial. Thousands of divers descend each year onto the soft coral walls and shipwrecks, but thankfully the offshore reefs and islands look like they have hardly had any tourism impact due to the flourishing habitats, which continue to seed the reefs with new life.

Getting there

Virtually all of the commercial airlines fly into Egypt, principally to Sharm el-Sheikh, Hurghada and Marsa Alam. There is also a significant number of tour operator-owned planes that fly tourists to their own resorts. As flying time is only around 4–5 hours from Europe, it is incredibly quick and easy to get to the Red Sea and have the maximum time available for your diving holiday.

Decompressing on the mooring line after a deep wreck dive.

You can also travel to Aqaba in Jordan and perhaps dive the famous *Cedar Pride* wreck and visit the incredible ruins of Petra before catching a ferry across the Gulf of Aqaba/Eilat to Nuweiba in the Sinai. Alternatively, you could fly into Eilat in Israel and cross over into Egypt at the border in Taba near the Coral Island.

Passport/Visa

A tourist visa for up to 30 days is required when visiting Egypt and this is usually paid for when you arrive at any of the Egyptian airports. It costs US$25 and is obtained from an approved bank kiosk in the terminal before you go to the Immigration counter. There is no need to use an agent to get a visa, but you can obtain one in advance from any Egyptian Consular office. However, British nationals travelling to Sharm el-Sheikh, Dahab, Nuweiba and Taba resorts for up to 15 days receive a free entry permission stamp upon arrival. If you intend to travel out of these areas or stay longer than 15 days, you must get a visa. Your passport should be valid for a minimum period of 6 months from the date of entry into Egypt.

Money

You can convert your dollars, pounds or euros at the airport, but most shops will give you local currency in change when you pay in foreign currency. Egyptian pounds are divided into 100 piastres or 1,000 millimes. The currency is designated as E£ in shops or on internet sites.

Transport

Transport is usually arranged by your tour operator who will have an agent waiting at the airport terminal for you and they will take you to your hotel or live-aboard dive boat in the port. Rental cars are available, but most visitors just use the local taxis to get you around on short journeys; always check out the price first! Your tour operator will also give you the pick-up times for when you are exiting the country. Remember that if you decide to take a further tour either by bus or by taxi that leaves the main tourist areas, you will have to take your passport with you and a full tourist visa.

Accommodation

A wide variety of accommodation is available and some seasoned travellers opt for renting a house, which they can all share to keep the costs down. Alternatively, there is a huge number of upmarket resorts situated along the coast that can be booked via your tour operator. Some of the larger dive centres have their own apartments and restaurants on site and of course, when staying on a live-aboard dive boat, you will be spending your week at sea and only having your last night on land in a resort.

Glossary of locally used names	
Abu	Father
Bommie	Single coral outcrop or coral head close to shore
Erg	Single coral head
Farsha	Deeper sunken reef not visible from the surface, usually from 15 m (50 ft)
Gota	Small part of a larger reef system
Habili	Arabic translation is 'unborn or pregnant', this is a reef that comes close to the surface, but starts around 3 m (10 ft)
Marsa	Sheltered bay
Ras	Head or headland
Sha'ab	Offshore reef system often with lagoons
Sharm	Bay or inlet

The Marine Environment

The Red Sea has a number of distinct ecosystems, all of which are accessible to sports divers of all levels of experience. There are distinct types of marine life to be found in all of the habitats and most species are adaptable to most of the environments. Many of the zones are designated as coastal habitats and the northern Red Sea with its shallow fringing reef close to large tourism enclaves clearly has the largest impact from tourists. Whilst a number of piers have been built over the shoreside reefs, these now make deeper water much more accessible and actually lessen the impact of tourism in the region. Most snorkelling is done along the edge of the fringing reef and has little or no impact on the ecosystem.

Glassy Sweepers are found in their thousands.

Open ocean

Whilst the Red Sea is in principal an 'enclosed' sea, it also has vast stretches of open water, with various converging currents carrying plankton-rich water throughout the region. Tiny sea mounts, rocky reefs and even shipwrecks become natural oases for attracting marine life, but there are also vast schools of pelagic fish, which patrol the open water. Jacks, barracuda, the mighty Whale Shark, pods of dolphins, porpoises and even large cetaceans use this watery highway to feed.

Mangrove forest

Some mangrove forests have been lost particularly along mainland Egypt's southern locations due to coastal developments. However, there are protected mangrove zones off the northern coast of Tiran Island and the superb mangrove forest at Ras Muhammed. This area covers almost a hectare and is one of the most important hatcheries for young fish and invertebrates in the Sinai Peninsula. A number of mangrove zones off the Sudan have fallen foul to nearby human populations where not only is their human waste a problem, but also the fact that their camels love to eat mangroves!

The mangroves' ecological importance includes:
• providing coastal protection from erosion
• trapping sediments
• consolidating the shoreline habitats
• providing nursery grounds and shelter for a number of marine organisms
• providing nesting and roosting sites for several avian fauna
• enriching the marine food web in the surrounding oligotrophic (nutrient-poor, oxygen-rich) water.

Seagrass beds

Seagrass beds are incredibly important to the entire Red Sea as they provide the principal food source for Dugong, as well as a number of turtles. Off the coast of Hurghada and Marsa Alam many of the marsas, or bays, have extensive seagrass meadows and these also act as hatcheries for fish, squid and cuttlefish that lay their eggs amongst them.

There are 11 different species of seagrass recorded from the entire Red Sea, with the most common being *Thalassia hemprichii*. Only seven species are found in the northern Red Sea, the other six being *Cymodacea rotundata; Cymodacea cerulatta; Halophila stipulacea; Halophila ovalis; Halodula uninervis* and *Thalassodendron ciliatum.* Their ecological importance includes the following:
• the roots hold sediment and prevent coastal erosion
• the leaves slow water movement and act as a filter for sewage
• they provide shelter and nurseries for many species of fish and invertebrate
• they are feeding grounds for both carnivores and herbivores
• they provide oxygen through photosynthesis
• they decompose organic matter

Reef Structures

Fringing reef

By far the most common reef structure in the northern Red Sea is the fringing reef, sometimes referred to as a shore reef. Virtually the entire southern Sinai has a fringing reef, where the corals grow out from the shoreline, with their top level just beneath the surface. During extreme low tides at the equinox, some of these corals may be exposed to the air. Fringing reefs have no intervening lagoon, which can act as a buffer to protect the reef from freshwater run-off, sedimentation or pollution; subsequently fringing reefs are most susceptible to this type of human impact. The two Brothers Islands have a fantastic fringing reef, which plummets into the depths.

Barrier reef

A barrier reef comprises extensive linear reef complexes, which run parallel to the shore and are separated from it by a (usually) shallow lagoon. One of the best barrier reefs in the Gulf of Suez is Sha'ab Ali, which has actually become more extensive and covers a large area of shallow water to the west of the Sinai Peninsula.

Patch reef

Patch reefs are found all over the northern Red Sea and are sometimes referred to as a micro-scaled combination of all the other reef types. Patch reefs are usually single or groups of isolated coral heads, which can be found quite independent from other nearby reefs, or they can extend out from either a barrier reef or a fringing reef. There are patch reefs in Sha'ab Ali, the Alternatives, Tiran Island, around Hurghada, nearby Marsa Alam and, in fact, most of the way down the Egyptian mainland coast.

Submerged seamounts

A seamount is an underwater mountain formed by volcanic activity. Some of these have broached the surface, such as the Brothers Islands; others, like Elphinstone, barely reach the surface and are more readily indicated by the rough water caused by waves crashing over the top.

Coral lagoons

In the context of coral reef typology, a lagoon is classified as either the strip of water between the land and the barrier reef or the enclosed area of water, which can be virtually surrounded by a coral reef. There are a number of superb coral lagoons in the northern Red Sea, such as off Sanafir, northern Tiran, Sha'ab Ali and Sha'ab Abu Nuhas. The latter in particular is superb.

Coral islands

There are a number of coral islands throughout the Red Sea, though fewer than you would think. Most of the offshore islands are, in fact, old limestone coral reefs sitting on top of ancient subterranean mountains. These have evolved through volcanic upheaval combined with the lowering of sea levels. However, there are true coral islands that have risen gradually at the same time as the sea level dropped. In time a small fringing reef develops around the edge giving it greater stability and protecting it from bad storms. The tops fill in with sand created from broken corals and fish debris.

Drop-offs

The Red Sea is famous for its vertical reef walls, which plummet from the surface to mind-boggling depths, formed where there was virtually no fresh

Pristine mangrove forests are still found all over the Red Sea.

water run-off or nearby rivers. These ancient coral reefs have formed over volcanic land pushed up over the millennia and are now covered in a very thin patina of healthy live corals. The strength of the surrounding currents also contributes to the formation of the walls. As the Red Sea is an extension of the Great Rift Valley, there is also extreme depth very close to shore and the wall at Ras Muhammed is one of the finest vertical coral walls you will ever encounter. However, the northern Red Sea also has stunning walls off the south and south-west corner of Tiran Island, Jackson Reef, Ras Umm Sid, Ras Zatar (near the inlet at Marsa Bureika at Ras Muhammed) as well as the offshore islands to the south.

Caves and caverns

Many of the fringing reefs are deeply pocked with small caves and caverns as coral growth combined with tidal movements have shaped the structure. Other caves have been formed through volcanic action and there are several large splits at Ras Muhammed where small earthquakes have cracked the old limestone shoreline. At Umm Qamar off eastern Hurghada there is a large cave entrance at around 30 m (100 ft) and just inside to the left, a fissure cleaves the old reef and allows access to a hidden world where no sunlight has been seen for hundreds of years.

At Dahab there is the famous blue hole (see page 50). Similarly on Woodhouse Reef in the Straits of Tiran there are several deep fissures. There are small caverns at Ras Muhammed, Big Brother Island and numerous other sites as well as a superb shore entry into a long cavern at Ras Umm Sid, nearby Sharm el-Sheikh.

Shipwrecks

Shallow reefs in the centre of shipping channels are the primary reason for ships running aground. As the sun starts to set and the Red Sea takes on an 'oily calm' appearance, all sights of hidden reefs just lurking below the surface disappear. There are shipwrecks dotted all around the Red Sea that have become enveloped in marine life.

Vertical walls are one of the main attractions for divers.

Motorbikes were part of the *Thistlegorm*'s cargo.

Life on the Coral Reef

The Red Sea reefs are host to over 1,000 types of invertebrate and 200 species of hard and soft coral. There are over 1,200 species of fish, of which 10 per cent are endemic to the region. The Red Sea is virtually enclosed with only a narrow opening at the Bab el-Mandeb Strait in Yemen. One would think that this would affect the coral growth, but with the deeper Red Sea creating upwellings and strong tidal movements through the Straits of Tiran, the coral reproduction is incredibly prolific and the reefs are constantly replenished by new growth.

There is very little commercial fishing in the Red Sea apart from the local Bedouin fishermen who patrol the shallow reefs of Sha'ab Ali, resulting in very large populations of reef fish, particularly around the exposed headland of Ras Muhammed, where, during the summer months, simply gigantic schools of snapper, grunt, barracuda, batfish, emperorfish, turtles and sharks congregate.

Green Turtles are the predominant species found on the Red Sea reefs and seagrass meadows, but Hawksbill Turtles also nest on the protected offshore islands. This latter species does create quite a bit of havoc on the reef as they eat soft leathery corals and large sponges, creating substantial scars on the colonies. This can, in turn, lead to algae colonization, which can ultimately kill the host, but such are the voracious appetites of the various species of wrasse that the algae are quickly kept in check, and the corals and sponges soon heal and reform.

Occasionally, much larger visitors come into the Red Sea; humpback whales and even a Blue Whale have been seen. However, it is the Whale Shark (*Rhynchodon typus*) that divers most love to see. Manta Rays also patrol the outer reefs and perhaps the rarest of all sightings is the Dugong or Sea Cow.

Parrotfish species are numerous on the reef and these, too, have an impact on the corals as they

Hermit Crab (*Dardanus pedunculatus*) inhabiting Spiny Murex Shell (*Murex tribulus*).

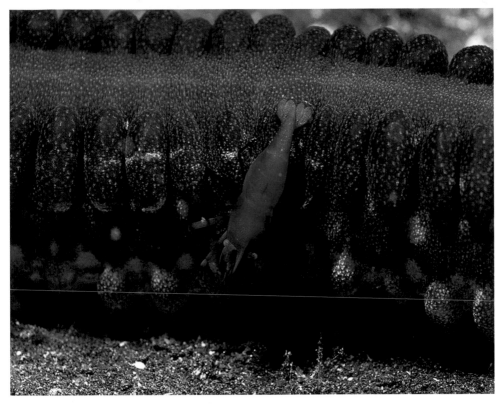

Emperor Shrimps are found on many different invertebrates.

eat the stony hard corals to digest the symbiotic algae that grow there. The coral excrement is ejected and helps to form the basis of the sandy beaches throughout the region. Like parrotfish, surgeonfish, wrasse and rabbitfish all feed on the reef; many smaller fish species catch plankton from the water column, other invertebrates patrol the coral recesses and these in turn are predated upon by small moray eels, groupers, lizardfish and lionfish.

Sea cucumbers, burrowing starfish and many molluscs inhabit the seabed, while even on vertical reef walls, there are always sandy shelves where turtles rest at night. These shelves collect sand debris and small species of invertebrate deposited by that great planktonic soup, developing small

and confined ecosystems that resemble the seabed.

Some fish species rely on their huge numbers for defence as the overall shape of their school is always shifting and changing. Smaller schooling species, such as the Red Sea Glassy Sweepers (*Parapriacanthus guentheri*), are usually found amidst the coral boulders or at the entrance of coral caverns. Around the outside of these schools there are always lionfish, grouper and squirrelfish. Squirrelfish in turn are predated upon by grouper. Larger fish also prefer schooling such as unicornfish, emperorfish, jacks, batfish and barracudas. This is hardly for defence as they are all large fish with perhaps only a shark as predator, but predatory fish just like to be sociable.

Reef Relationships

Cleaning stations

Cleaning stations are found on every small section of coral reef in tropical and temperate waters. These are areas where larger fish come to be 'cleaned' of parasites and of any diseased scales or skin by a number of different reef inhabitants including various species of goby and blenny, and numerous types of shrimp for whom this is food. It is common to see predators and prey lining up at cleaning stations, all enmity forgotten. This social truce is integral to the survival of the fish populations on the reef. These fish are not just individuals struggling to survive, they are part of an incredibly complex, integrated structure, which works to a firm set of guidelines that they all follow.

The most common of the cleaner wrasse is *Labroides dimidiatus*. These small fish – up to 10 cm (3 in) long – often work in pairs all over the hard stony corals waiting for fish to approach their protected area of the reef. They advertise their trade by dancing in a distinctive pattern of jerking up-and-down movements.

Camouflage

Bottom dwellers, such as the Crocodile Fish and stonefish, rely on their superb camouflage, lying motionless and waiting for passing prey to get close enough to their mouths. Stargazers hide virtually submerged with their upturned mouths just below the surface; stingrays settle onto the seabed with only their eyes visible and many small crabs attach small pieces of coral or sponge to their shells, claws and legs to disguise their shape.

Various species of butterflyfish have 'extra' eyes in their colouration and when danger nears, they turn sideways to present a supposedly much larger visage to the hunter. Other fish species are just curiously shaped to confuse predators, so that they do not look like fish at all. Undoubtedly one of the best camouflage artists is the octopus. Not only can it change colour to match its surroundings, but it can also change its shape configuration and have small lumpy bits all over, to more closely resemble corals.

Cleaner wrasses are active in all areas of the reef.

Painted Lizardfish lie in wait under the sand.

Frogfish are masters of camouflage.

Mimicry

The Red Sea has a number of very well-known mimics, in particular the voracious and predatory Fang-tooth Blenny (*Aspidontus taeniatus*), which is almost identical to the Blue-streaked Cleaner Wrasse (*Labroides dimidiatus*). This false cleanerfish copies both the dance and appearance of the cleaner wrasse, allowing it to trick the other fish and take a quick nip of skin out of its prey.

Juvenile Rock-mover Wrasses (*Novaculichthys taeniourus*) move about the coral rubble like a fluttering dead leaf. Some frogfish resemble bits of sponge and even appear to show the inhalation and exhalation tubes. *Solenostomus cyanopterus* and *Solenostomus paradoxus*, both species of ghost pipefish, so resemble their habitats that they are virtually indistinguishable to the human eye. Small flounders can resemble flatworms and harmless eels may look like venomous sea snakes, all to add confusion into the hunter and hunted equation.

Symbiosis

Harmonized living underwater is about hosts and mutual friendship, it's about being able to blend in with your surroundings and not predate on your neighbours unless they invade your living/eating space. The underwater world has had centuries in which to refine these relationships and nowhere else in nature are these symbiotic relationships so abundant. Symbiosis can refer to any of several beneficial or harmful living arrangements between two different species including commensalism, mutualism and parasitism. Members in these relationships are called symbionts.

Perhaps the most surprising symbiosis is that of the algae that produce the colour pigmentation in the lining of coral animals' tissue. Their interesting shades of green, orange, blue and brown are all the result of an algae. It is this algae and coral animal tissue that so attract parrotfish and various wrasse which feed on the corals. This algae is also the first indication of coral bleaching. When the sea temperature rises too high, too fast, the algae is expelled or dies off and the coral's bleached white skeleton is then exposed. If the sea temperature does not reduce quickly, the coral may die.

Commensalism is the association between two or more individuals in the interests of nutrition, shelter, support, locomotion or transportation. In general terms, one of the species involved is able to benefit from the association – the commensal (from the Latin meaning 'sharing the same table') – and the other, the host, is unaffected. The commensal may be external, such as the remora, or internal, such as the micro-organisms found in the digestive tracts of animals. Many hosts can be found without commensals, but no commensals are ever found without their hosts.

Many species have become so adapted to commensal life that they have evolved into a specific colour pattern or shape entirely to match the host species, such as the dorsal fin of the remora or suckerfish, which has been adapted into a suction disc. These fish attach themselves to pelagic hosts such as sharks, turtles and Manta Rays. Travelling the oceans, they steal morsels of food from their hosts' mouths if necessary. They also act as 'cleaners' to some of the larger sea creatures but more often than not they appear to be opportunistic feeders and along for the free ride.

The Whip Coral Goby (*Bryaninops yongei*) gets its name from the coral on which it lives. The mated

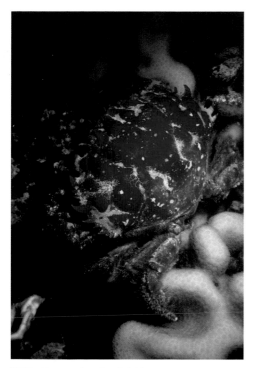

Coral crabs are only active at night.

pair spend all their lives travelling the whip coral and eating the larger bits of plankton which are caught within it. They also eat the coral polyps and lay their demersal eggs on the bared stalk.

One of the most interesting commensal associations on the reef is between several species of sand goby and a variety of shrimps. The almost-blind shrimps' primary role is burrow maintenance. Constantly excavating their holes, they are advised when it is safe to emerge with their excavated material by a flick of the goby's tail. When danger threatens, the fish dives into the hole and so protects the shrimp. The Shrimp Goby *Amblyeleotris steinitzi* is the most common in the Red Sea and is readily seen in most shallow coral lagoons.

Sponges, sea cucumbers, nudibranchs, corals, anemones, sea urchins, clams, feather starfish and Basket Starfish all have various specialized hitchhikers or commensals. These can be small worms, shrimps, crabs, anemones, sponges, tunicates, molluscs or fish. Many of these are very small, living on or around a much larger host for protection, but there are others who obviously enjoy mutual co-operation and other beneficial arrangements.

Mutualism is the association between two different species of animal in which each is benefitted. Mutualistic arrangements are most likely to occur between species with very different living requirements.

Cleaner shrimps and cleaner wrasse fulfil a vital function of reef life and are mutually beneficial to the health of the host species by removing parasites or decaying and dead skin and scales. Classic case studies in the Red Sea have looked at the Imperial Shrimp (*Pereclimenes imperator*) and its host species the Spanish Dancer nudibranch (*Hexabranchus sanguineus*).

These tiny shrimp live with immunity on this large nudibranch. In return for its protection, the shrimp keeps the nudibranch clean of parasites and waste products and will also clean other invertebrates in the vicinity. *Pereclimenes imperator* can also be found on different nudibranchs and sea cucumbers. The Crown-of-thorns Starfish (*Acanthaster planci*) has a similarly related shrimp, the Starfish Shrimp (*Pereclimenes soror*).

The classic symbol of living in harmony is that between the Anemonefish and its host anemone. There are three species found in the Red Sea but *Amphiprion bicinctus* is the only endemic species and the one most commonly seen. This fish secretes mucus on its skin that renders it 'invisible' to the anemone's stinging cells or nematocysts. In return for this anonymity, the Anemonefish protects its host from predators and feeds on any scraps left over by its partner. Anemonefish also lay their eggs on the bare rock or coral under the protective reach of the anemone's tentacles. Another, yet rarer find in the Red Sea is the Red-spotted Porcelain Crab (*Neopetrolisthes maculatus*). This brightly coloured crab hangs onto the fleshy underparts of the anemone and is also able to scuttle amongst the stinging tentacles and may even enter the mouth and stomach with impunity.

Parasitism is the relationship between two plants or animals in which one benefits at the expense of the other, without actually killing the host. A relationship where the host is specifically killed is called parasitoidism.

In the Red Sea, there is a species of isopod or sea louse of the *Anilocra* family, which attaches itself to a number of fish species, including squirrelfish, small grouper and even Anemonefish, where it actively feeds on its host species and may eventually kill it. Much harder to find is the

Why reef creatures are red at night
Curiously, many nocturnal reef fish are coloured in shades of red, which makes them instantly visible in the light of our dive torches. Why red at night? Red fish appear red on the surface or when struck by torchlight because they reflect red light from the spectrum and absorb the other colours. However, as you go deeper or when the sun disappears at night, there is less red light to reflect off the creatures. The quality and type of light changes as you descend and the colour red disappears at around 1.8 m (6 ft); in fact the entire spectrum of light changes as you descend until only the blues are still visible. Red light also has the longest wavelength and therefore the least amount of energy visible in the spectrum.

When there is no white light, the creatures appear black and virtually disappear making them much harder to see by predators.

tiny parasite *Myzostoma fuscomaculatum*, which latches onto one of the tentacles and takes on the shape and colouration of the crinoid.

Night and day
The Red Sea has some incredible night diving, during which the more common reef fish hide in the coral recesses for protection, whilst the nocturnal fish now stir and are soon swimming all over the coral reef. The number of invertebrates that come out at night is simply astonishing and you are able to catch the fluorescent green eyes of the small shrimps and the luminous eye patches of *Photoblepharon*. Then, as your eyes adjust to swimming in closer proximity to the reef, your torchlight soon picks out all the weird and wonderful marine creatures that you never saw during the day. There are a few species of frogfish; Spanish Dancer nudibranchs, which undulate in the water column in front of you; basket starfish with tiny commensal shrimps; Crinoids or feather starfish, also with symbiotic shrimps, squat lobsters and crabs; Long-spined Sea Urchins (*Diadema paucispinum*) and, of course, the multi-coloured soft corals. At night

Although rarely seen, the Triton's Trumpet is the main threat to Crown-of-Thorns Starfish.

the colours reflected by your torchlight are simply stunning and it is the reds, oranges and yellows that immediately come to light.

Red sea rarities

Many divers do not realise the number of quite rare species that are found in the Red Sea and these are certainly testimony to the tidal vagaries and planktonic shift across the oceans. Below is just a small representation of species that continue to be discovered in the Red Sea.

The Sea Moth or the Little Dragonfish (*Eurypegasus draconis*) has been found as far north as Eilat. Living on a sandy seabed it can 'walk' along the substrate on adapted pelvic fins and has a curious long snout. Similarly, another rarity amongst the scorpionfish is the Red Sea Walkman (*Inimicus filamentosus*), which lives amidst the coral rubble.

Two species of ghost pipefish are recorded from the Red Sea, the Ornate Ghost Pipefish (*Solenostomus paradoxus)* and the Robust Ghost Pipefish (*Solenostomus cyanopterus*).

The Porcelain Crab (*Neopetrolisthes maculatus*) can be found from the Red Sea to Australia and has the most charming way of feeding for microscopic plankton by wafting large, net-like appendages into the current.

Pairs of the Whip Coral Goby (*Bryaninops yongei*) (see page 26) share their tiny, pencil-thin home with a few different species of shrimp, which are even harder to see as they blend in with their surroundings so well.

Of the shrimp family, one of the most exotic of all is the Imperial Shrimp (*Pereclimenes imperator*).

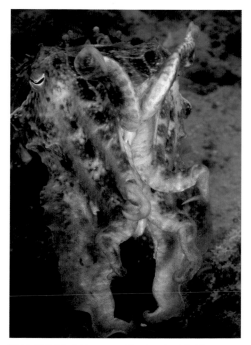

The cuttlefish is more common than imagined, but its camouflage is superb.

Threats

The main threat in modern times to the fragility of the Red Sea is from accidental (or otherwise) shipwrecks. Almost every year some ship or supertanker runs aground in the Red Sea, perhaps through navigational error, bad luck and timing, laziness in taking short cuts, ineptitude or sadly (as I have witnessed) insurance scams. A multi-ton tanker ploughing into a reef crest inevitably destroys huge swathes of the delicate marine corals. The resultant oil spill can smother corals, wash up on beaches, be ingested by larger marine animals and birds, and cause catastrophic changes to the ecosystem.

Coral bleaching rarely affects the corals of the northern Red Sea as the sea temperature is fairly equable all year round. There are localized threats from the Crown-of-thorns Starfish (*Acanthaster planci*) where larger adult starfish can kill *Acropora* table corals, but this is fairly negligible. These starfish are only responding to the over-abundance of hard coral reproduction and as always, nature tries to find a way to keep the balance even.

Thankfully the Red Sea is fed with cold water upwellings, and a very vibrant and healthy coral system, so that any damaged corals will repair themselves and even damaged reefs soon have a patina of new algae growth, before the harder corals start to recolonize.

Undoubtedly, over-diving in prime locations is a serious threat to the ecosystem, but thankfully there are management plans in place to help this. However, there are always rogue diving operators who care little for rules and regulations and will constantly try to gain a small profit at the expense of all others.

Development has forever changed the coastline with the addition of piers, marinas, harbours and reclaimed areas of fringing reef to support tourism. The main threat appears to be the lack of sewage treatment plants to handle the increased waste from coastal hotels and resorts. Offshore oilspills from oil rigs are also apparently fairly regular and there appears to be a real lack of awareness of emergency procedures.

Clingfish spend their lives hiding amongst sea urchin spines.

The United Nations Environment Programme (UNEP) has warned of what is happening to the Red Sea: *"The major threats to the marine environment of the Red Sea and Gulf of Aden are related to land-based activities. These include urbanisation and coastal development (for example, dredge and fill operations), industries including power and desalination plants and refineries, recreation and tourism, waste water treatment facilities, power plants, coastal mining and quarrying activities, oil bunkering and habitat modification such as the filling and conversion of wetlands."*

Marine Conservation

Overall, the reefs are in remarkable condition considering the local pressures that are placed on them. The mooring buoy system allows for some sites to have a rest, whilst others are opened up nearby thus spreading the load of visitor numbers. Political pressures and internal conflict have surprisingly also helped the reefs to recover.

Whilst this problem certainly affects the tourism sector, there is also a winner and this is the health of the coral reefs.

The King Abdullah University of Science & Technology (KAUST) has reported that the reefs of the Red Sea are amongst the healthiest in the world, but are, of course, still vulnerable to many different types of environmental threat as mentioned above. The Red Sea Environmental Centre (RSEC) runs a field school in the Sinai at Dahab and offer students the chance of hands-on conservation awareness.

The oldest marine conservation organization is HEPCA founded in 1992. All of the responsible diving centres are members and the association is very active in reef monitoring and conservation policies; they work closely with the Egyptian Environmental Affairs Agency. HEPCA launched a campaign in 2015, garnering the support of local Egyptian government in the area, to ban the use of plastic bags at supermarkets. In the past

Marine conservation measures ensure healthy coral reefs.

waste bags have blown from landfill sites in the mountains into the sea and these have caused problems for the corals, fish and turtles, which inadvertently mistake the bags for their favourite prey – jellyfish.

The Regional Organization for the Conservation of the Environment of the Red Sea and Gulf of Aden (PERSGA) is an intergovernmental body dedicated to the conservation of the coastal and marine environments found in the Red Sea, Gulf of Aqaba, Gulf of Suez, Suez Canal and Gulf of Aden surrounding the Socotra Archipelago and nearby waters. PERSGA's member states include: Djibouti, Egypt, Jordan, the Kingdom of Saudi Arabia, Somalia, Sudan and Yemen. This intergovernmental association appears to be working, but in most areas, it is local hands-on conservation policies that are the most effective.

The Marine Twilight Zone Research and Exploration programme (MTRX) was set up in 2003 by the Interuniversity Institute for Marine Sciences of Eilat to conduct research on the deep, coral-reef systems of the northern Red Sea.

The Ras Muhammed Marine National Park was created in 1983 by the EEAA (Egyptian Environmental Affairs Agency), who established the reserve to protect the area from any urban sprawl from Sharm el-Sheikh. However, it was actually a few years after that before any type of legislation started to appear. The park is located 12 km (7½ miles) from Sharm el-Sheikh and spans an area of 480 km² (185 sq. miles) including 135 km² (52 sq. miles) of land. The reserve has also been expanded outwards to include the islands of Tiran and Sanafir to the north-east. Ras Muhammed Park has almost a hectare (2½ acres) of mangrove forest, which covers a narrow channel near the southernmost point of the Sinai Peninsula and is an important nursery for reef fish and invertebrates.

Good buoyancy is essential whenever you are near the reef.

Guidelines issued by the national parks of Egypt in relation to the behaviour of individuals and businesses in the marine protectorates aim to restrict any intentional or unintentional damage to the environment. The guidelines include the following advice:

• Mooring buoys are installed to protect corals, which would otherwise be damaged by the use of anchors.

• Divers can contribute by not touching or breaking corals. The usual rule to help enforce this is by not wearing gloves underwater.

• Fish feeding and bottom fishing upset the equilibrium of the reef. Do not feed or fish on the coastline.

• Improve your buoyancy and look but don't touch! PADI speciality courses, such as Peak Performance Buoyancy and Underwater Naturalist, are available to improve your awareness of the environment and help you interact with it in a mutually beneficial way. Resting, standing or walking on a coral surface damages the fragile tissue surface of the coral animal. Exposed to bacterial attack and disease, it will often not recover from this impact. Avoid walking on the reef. Use the floating jetties or marked reef access points to enter the water.

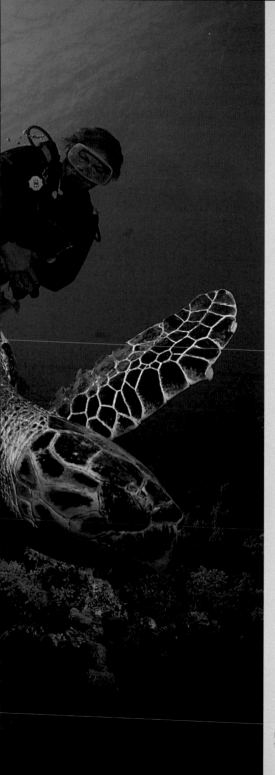

Diving and Snorkelling in the Red Sea

If you are thinking of scuba diving for the first time, then the Red Sea is the perfect location and the closest tropical reef to all of Europe. All the top dive centres have multi-lingual, highly qualified instructors to help you achieve your goal.

Lesley and a Green Turtle off Jackson Reef, which is perfect for snorkelling and diving.

Health and Safety

Pre-travel

Medical fitness

Undoubtedly it does help if you have a fair level of fitness when diving in the Red Sea as you may well encounter strong currents whilst underwater, often running in different directions on the same dive, particularly if you are diving around the tip of a reef where converging currents can sometimes be punishing.

All qualified divers will have an up-to-date medical certificate as part of their diving licence and whilst this is not a requirement to dive, it does make good sense to keep this current, particularly if you have had a lay-off from diving for any length of time. The water may be clear, warm and calm, but the dangers are the same as for every large body of water.

Vaccinations and malaria

Malaria does not appear to be a problem, although there are instances of yellow fever further south in the mainland towards the Sudan. Hepatitis A and typhoid immunizations are always worth keeping up to date, and there are websites which you can check, just in case there are any increasing health threats.

Lionfish have venom on the tips of their fin spines.

Stomach problems

To prevent any stomach problems, drink only bottled water, avoid icecreams, or ice in your drinks, and eat only peeled fruits and vegetables. Always wash your hands and take anti-bacterial wipes or sprays to use whenever you are out and about.

Sunburn

Sunburn is always a problem and with virtually zero humidity, your sweat just wicks from your skin. This combined with those nice, cooling sea breezes, leave you unaware of the strength of the sun's rays. Always wear a strong and waterproof sunscreen and re-apply regularly throughout the day. Most people suffer on their first couple of days as they forget to apply sunscreen on their shoulders and back when just snorkelling along the edge of the reef. Out of the water, wear a hat and sunglasses as well as protective clothing.

Dehydration

Dehydration can increase your susceptibility to decompression sickness (DCS), so it is vitally important to keep hydrated throughout your holiday. Drink plenty of water, fruit juice, etc. and perhaps take re-hydration sachets with you. Alcohol also increases the risk of dehydration and DCS, so when diving regularly it is good advice not to take alcohol.

Seasickness

Seasickness can be a problem when either using the day boats or spending the week on a live-aboard. Day boats are much smaller, more cramped for space and may not be as stable in the water as you would like, particularly when moored for long periods on a dive site where the constant rocking and jostling from other boats can be quite unpleasant. Live-aboard boats are more stable, but always take seasickness remedies that suit your constitution and take them in plenty of time to avoid illness. It is usual to also take this preventative remedy when coming back on land after spending a week or two at sea!

Medical treatment

The Hyperbaric Chamber in Sharm el-Sheikh has an excellent medical centre with full-time staff and is able to assist with most complaints or accidents. More serious treatment will always be routed through Cairo.

Hyperbaric chamber

The Recompression Chamber was first opened in Sharm el-Sheikh in 1993, initially funded through US AID but is now under the Ministry of Tourism in Egypt. Located near the main jetty at Sharm el-Mena in Sharm, there is also a very good medical centre and most visitors will use this facility in preference to anything else.

Insurance

Treatment in the recompression chamber is not covered by conventional healthcare insurance policies, so please remember to carry a valid diver accident insurance (such as through DAN), whenever you travel to dive outside your home country. Most holiday companies do offer insurance for diving holidays as an additional premium.

Hazardous marine life

Like all seas everywhere, there are always hazardous critters that divers and snorkellers may encounter underwater. Tropical waters have more than their fair share and the Red Sea is no exception.

Stonefish

A master at camouflage, a stonefish will basically just sit still usually in a coral rubble seabed in water less that 18 m (60 ft) deep. Once ensconced in a favourite hunting site, the fish just

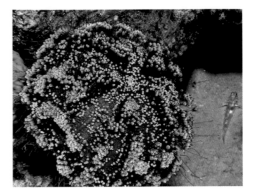
This sea urchin has extremely venomous spines.

waits until its prey swims close by its upturned mouth. Their sedentary nature and superb camouflage make them virtually disappear, until you accidentally put your hand on one or kneel where you shouldn't. The venomous spines in its dorsal fin can inflict excruciating pain and medical help must be sought as soon as possible.

Lionfish

A cousin of the stonefish, there are a few different species found in the Red Sea, the most common of which is *Pterois volitans*. Lionfish loiter around schools of Glassy Sweepers in small caverns, usually hanging upside down under a coral ledge. They have venomous spines on the tips of their fins that inflict an extremely painful sting. A combination of cortisone, anti-histamine and immersion in hot water then freezing cold water helps.

Stingrays and electric rays

Most people are now well aware of the stinging barb found in the tail of stingrays and have enough sense to keep clear. However, there are times when you may be unaware of them hiding below the sand and, if they are threatened or cornered, they may be frightened into raising their tail and exposing their barb. Immerse the affected area in hot water with added vinegar. Electric rays are another matter, as they are usually hidden under the sand, again waiting for prey to come along. If you touch one of these, they can send a massive electric shock through your body up to 220 volts.

Sea urchins

Sea urchin spines are quite fragile and are easily broken off in the skin, particularly those of the long-spined sea urchin. The Flower Urchin (*Toxopneustes pileolus*) is one of the most frequently encountered, though well camouflaged, and has numerous venomous pedicellariae amidst the spines that look like little flowers. The Red Sea Urchin (*Mesocentrotus francisanus*) is another stinging sea urchin with small white venom sacks at the end of its spines. A nocturnal species, they come out at night and are often found clinging underneath a coral outcrop. During a night dive, divers should keep clear of these areas as exhaust air bubbles can dislodge the sea urchin and it may land on you with devastating effect. Immerse the affected area in hot water with added vinegar.

Cnidarians

This all-encompassing family includes the closely related corals, hydroids, anemones and jellyfish. The name cnidarian literally means 'stinging creature'. All of them have stinging cells or nematocysts, which they can fire into their prey to paralyse it before ingestion. Jellyfish are very close to corals and are, in fact, the free-swimming medusa form of the family; anemones and coral polyps are the fixed form. Most varieties of jellyfish are harmless; of the 2,000 species, only around 70 are seriously harmful to us. However, during night dives, Box Jellyfish (*Carukia barnesi*) can be found swimming near the surface and are attracted to the dive boat's lights. They deliver an extremely painful sting.

Some corals also have stinging cells as well as fire corals, which, though not a true coral (they are hydroids), are covered in minute hairs that easily penetrate the skin. Shipwrecks and nearshore conditions suit fire corals, so care must be taken.

The feather-like hydroids, which are soft in structure and waft gently in the current, can also pack a powerful sting. Some hermit crabs also carry hydroids as part of their defence mechanism, so keep your distance.

Crown-of-thorns Starfish

The Crown-of-thorns Starfish (*Acanthaster planci*), is the only venomous starfish that we know of in the Red Sea. It can have around 21 arms all tipped with venomous spines that can easily penetrate a wetsuit and skin. Local painful swelling, nausea and vomiting are common, so take care whenever you are close to one. Immerse the affected area in hot water with added vinegar.

Cone shells

The general rule is never to collect any creatures or shells whilst underwater. Cone shells in particular have a very powerful harpoon, which can easily penetrate the skin if you are not careful. Seek medical care if affected.

Sharks

I am reluctant to include sharks in this list, as they are such a maligned species, particularly in the Red Sea. There are a large number of sharks to be found in the region, from the largest fish in the sea, the Whale Shark (*Rhinchodon typus*), to smaller cat sharks. Oceanic Whitetip (*Carcharhinus longimanus*), Thresher (*Alopias vulpinus*), Sandbar (*Carcharhinus plumbeus*) and hammerhead sharks to name but a few, can be found. Most of the sharks are quite timid and are usually found on the deeper reefs or in stronger currents.

Equipment

Diving and snorkelling

Having your own equipment is always important, but for many backpackers this is not an option due to weight restrictions. Thankfully all of the dive centres have superb rental equipment. However, it is always better to have your own mask, snorkel and fins as they are specific to you, your facial features, your comfort for wearing and foot size – whether it is with a full foot fin or an adjustable fin with straps to wear with hard-soled booties.

Most visiting divers tend to wear a 'shorty suit', but this is not entirely practical, as it is always better to wear full protection to avoid accidental stings from hydroids or floating particulate in the water column. Winter water temperatures really require a 7 mm wetsuit or semi-dry suit, but for extended diving in the winter months, many European divers bring drysuits. Getting cold in the water, together with a chilly wind on the surface can give you problems that you least expect in a 'tropical' sea.

Dive centres and boats all have air/nitrox tanks available and these are often included in the cost of your holiday. Nitrox (oxygen-enriched air) can cost more and you must bring your nitrox qualification card with you. You will be responsible for checking the mix of the air before every dive.

Most tourists' first look at the underwater wonders of the Red Sea is by snorkelling. Even just stepping into the sea from the shore will introduce you to a world of tiny colourful fish all around you. Armed with just a mask and snorkel, you will be able to explore the near shore without the need for any protective wear, other than sunscreen but it is important to always wear hard-soled boots when walking along the shore before entering or exiting the water. Here you may well encounter sea urchins whose very sharp and fragile spines can easily break off in our unprotected skin.

Emperor Divers have the full range of rental dive equipment.

Underwater Photography

Underwater photography is so much more an option for everyone nowadays with the availability of mass-market digital cameras. Surprising and rare animal behaviour has been caught for the first time by tourists with a Go-Pro. Many of the smaller, lightweight, digital cameras are also waterproof down several metres and are perfect for snorkellers, as these cameras do not need to be in a waterproof housing.

For those who take their underwater photography more seriously, the two main types are wide-angle photography and close-up or macro photography. The benefits of wide-angle photography are that it puts other divers in the frame and can create exciting backdrops perhaps beside a steep drop-off or shipwreck.

Wide-angle application
- Cliff and reef drop-off panoramas
- Exteriors of shipwrecks
- Interiors of shipwrecks, caves and caverns
- Divers in action
- Divers and fish/animal interaction
- Wide-angle flash and flash-fill techniques
- Large fish and mammals
- Close-focus attention
- Available light and silhouettes

Macro photography is more specialized, where the lens is placed much closer to the subject to give you a magnified view. Once you are confident with this type of photography and are not stressing any of the critters, you will quickly find it is the most rewarding, as your flash will pick up the vibrant colours of the subject matter and it opens up a whole new world of tiny animals and plants not normally seen during average diving conditions.

Benefits of macro photography
- A different perspective
- High magnification
- Maximum colour saturation
- Sharp focus
- Ease of learning the technique
- Can be done anywhere, under almost any conditions
- Easiest to use on night dives
- Greatest return for the investment
- PADI offer courses in underwater photography and marine biology as part of your training and these can greatly enhance your knowledge and experience whilst underwater.

Beginner's guide to obtaining successful underwater photographs
- Approach one photographic technique or problem at a time. Don't try to do everything at once.
- View the technical details recorded electronically on your photographs to find out which settings are best for which subject.
- Keep your flash or strobe well away from the subject and camera (unless you are working in a macro situation). Position the flash at the top left (and right if using two flash) of the camera so that the light makes an angle of 45 degrees to the subject axis.
- Pre-aim the flash out of the water first to obtain the optimum reading in order to counter the effects of light refraction.
- Find the aperture that produces the most consistent results. Next time you take a photograph, take additional shots either side of this aperture (one stop lower and one stop higher). This is called bracketing and will take care of subjects with different brightnesses.
- Note the position of the sun when you enter the water, as you may wish to use it to create back-lit shots to add depth and interest.
- Get as close to your subject as possible, close-ups have the most impact and better colour saturation.
- Never take a photograph below you, always shoot horizontally or upwards.

Reeta Tunney uses superb buoyancy to get close to photographic subjects.

Inside the mouth of a cavern is a perfect spot for photographing Glassy Sweepers.

- You can pre-set your focus and allow the subject and yourself to approach each other gently and sympathetically.
- Try to take photographs in clear water and bright sunshine.
- Never use the flash when the flash and camera to subject distance is greater than one-fifth of the underwater visibility, e.g. if the visibility is 5 m (16½ ft), focus and use the flash at only 1 m (3¼ ft), that will cut down the reflection from suspended particulate (backscatter).
- Set your camera to the fastest aperture that the flash will synchronize to (unless using an automatic-housed system).
- Attend an underwater photography instruction course.
- Do not rely on the 'automatic' setting on the camera and expect your computer skills to rectify any problems with poorly exposed or composed photographs.
- Be ruthless. Really, the only way you learn is by self-criticism – it is important to learn from your mistakes, so by using the live-view screen on your camera, you should be able to look and learn as you go along.

Video

Video has undoubtedly gained enormous popularity through social media sites and literally thousands of hours of video are uploaded daily, most of it poorly executed. However, there are times when a simply stunning and spectacular underwater event is recorded for the first time. The new style Go-pro type of action video camera is perfectly suited for this type of photography, and for most divers, this camera has become an additional and necessary piece of their diving equipment.

Certification and Experience

Diving

There many different types of scuba diving certification available. These are usually dependent on the country you live in and what is seen to be the easier option. In the UK there is the Sub-Aqua Association (SAA), British Sub-Aqua Club (BSAC), Scottish Sub-Aqua Club (SSAC), International Association of Nitrox and Technical Divers (IANTD) and Professional Association of Diving Instructors International (PADI). In Europe the main agency is the Confédération Mondiale des Activités Subaquatiques (CMAS), but you can also be certified through Scuba Schools International (SSI) and PADI.

For many first-time divers, it is easy to sign up for a PADI course whilst on holiday and this 'Open water Diver' programme will take only a few days of your time. Additional training will take more time (and money), so for many it makes sense to do all of the written and pool work before the holiday. Through a referral system, you can then complete your dive training in the sea with a minimum of fuss. You can continue with your training all the way up to Diving Instructor and be qualified in the use of mixed gasses and rebreathers.

Snorkelling

You really do not need any experience to snorkel, although there are some junior training groups. It is assumed that if you are snorkelling in the open ocean, you have some level of competency and are a reasonably good swimmer just in case you do get into difficulty. Having your own mask, snorkel and fins is essential as you know that they fit well and are comfortable. Please remember to wear either strong sun-screen or a protective 'skin' if possible.

A well organized and tidy dive boat.

Diving Facilities

There are quite a few options available in the Red Sea and these include independent dive centres, concessionary dive centres attached to hotels and resorts, specific diving schools, such as Red Sea Diving College based in Na'ama Bay, and live-aboard dive boats.

Dive centres

Nearly all of the independent dive centres have training facilities and multi-lingual instructors, and all are able to teach the PADI system. Centres such as the Red Sea College, Sinai Divers, Emperor Divers, Sinai College, Camel and Oonasdivers have superb reputations, and all of them also offer accommodation and day or live-aboard dive boats. Shore diving is also an option for everyone and there are still a number of very good shore-based dive sites.

Day boats

All of the independent dive centres, instruction centres and hotel concessions offer day-boat diving. These boats are often quite small and can become crowded with tourists. Sadly, unless you are travelling with a group of other divers whom you know, you may well end up on a boat of divers with mixed ability and the dive crew on board will generally tailor the dive to those with the least experience. Try to take a buddy with you of the same qualification and experience as yourself, as you should be able to dive further away from the madding crowd and enjoy more time underwater. (Buddies also make great photographic models underwater!)

Live-aboards

By far the most popular way of diving the Red Sea is on a live-aboard dive boat. Guests are picked up at the airport and whisked to the waiting boat. Once rooms are allocated and everyone is settled in, a briefing will take place outlining the itinerary (weather-dependent), and which reefs and wrecks will be visited. The guides will also find out whether anyone will be doing further training whilst on board. Nitrox or air will

Emperor Divers have both day boats and live-aboards.

Most of the Sinai dive boats leave from Sharm el-Sheikh.

be offered, with nitrox usually at a premium. Other than nitrox, alcohol is the only other commodity that may cost you anything on board (apart from the obligatory T-shirts, etc.). All food, soft drinks, diving and transfers are taken care of in your package.

There is a huge number of travel companies who run very successful live-aboard operations that will traverse almost the entire Red Sea. However, most concentrate around the northern Red Sea, Straits of Tiran and Sinai Peninsula. Sharm el-Sheikh is the obvious epicentre of all this boat traffic and across on the mainland, Hurghada is another large base for live-aboards and day boats. There are increasing numbers of operators further south around Marsa Alam where they are able to travel with ease to the furthest of the Red Sea reefs.

Tours will vary in length, but usually last a week, with your final night in a hotel on shore to allow the dive boat to get ready for the next group of passengers. The beauty of the live-aboard is its flexibility, as you can tailor the diving to the weather and your needs. Most of the northern boats will include the *Thistlegorm* wreck, Ras Muhammed and the Straits of Tiran as part of their regular tour, but when you have the time to explore you should be able to travel further north to Shag Rock and across to Sha'ab Abu Nuhas, which has a handful of superb wrecks.

Whip Coral Gobies are a delight to find.

43

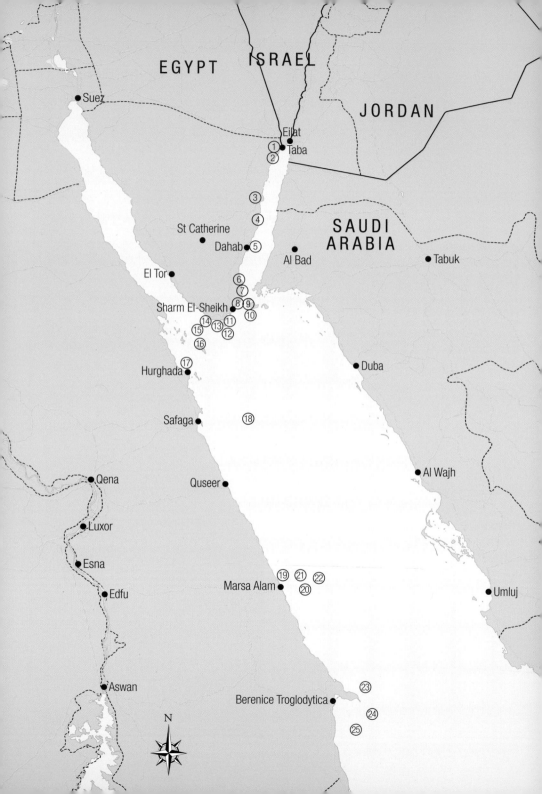

EGYPT

ISRAEL

JORDAN

Suez

Eilat
①
Taba
②

③

④

St Catherine
Dahab ⑤

SAUDI
ARABIA

Al Bad

Tabuk

El Tor

⑥
⑦
Sharm El-Sheikh ⑧⑨
⑩
⑭ ⑪
⑮ ⑬
⑫
⑯

Hurghada ⑰

Duba

Safaga

⑱

Quseer

Al Wajh

Qena

Luxor

Esna

Edfu

Marsa Alam ⑲ ㉑ ㉒
㉔

Umluj

Aswan

N

Berenice Troglodytica

㉓

㉔

㉕

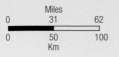

Miles
0   31   62
0   50   100
Km

Guide to Dive Sites

This chapter presents my selection of the best sites from literally hundreds of other fantastic places nearby. They have been chosen for their excessive marine life ensuring dives of spectacular quality. There are a few other wrecks that need mentioning in the southern reaches of the Red Sea. Ten km (6 miles) south of Marsa Alam are the remains of the *El* or *Al Qaher*, a former British Zambezi class destroyer. Further south and 68 km (48 miles) from Marsa Alam is the *Hamada*, which can be dived from the shore at Abu Ghosan in only a maximum depth of 18 m (60 ft). Even further south and 24 km (15 miles) north of Ras Banas near Hamata the SS *Turbo* lies in depths of only 18–28 m (60–95 ft).

Key to highlights at each site

![shark]	Shark
![turtle]	Turtle
![macro]	Macro (i.e small creatures)
![schools]	Schools of fish
![ray]	Ray
![coral]	Coral
![softcoral]	Soft coral
![wreck]	Wreck
![dolphin]	Dolphin
![pelagics]	Large pelagics
![dugong]	Dugong

Maps showing location of dive sites.

KEY TO DIVING SITES
1. Taba
2. Coral Island
3. Nuweiba
4. Ras Abu Galum
5. Dahab
6. The Gardens
7. The Tower
8. Ras Umm Sid
9. Straits of Tiran (Gordon Reef; Thomas Reef)
10. Straits of Tiran (Woodhouse Reef; Jackson Reef)
11. Ras Zatar
12. Ras Muhammad
13. The Alternatives
14. Sha'ab Ali
15. Shag Rock
16. Sha'ab Abu Nuhas
17. El Gouna Hurghada
18. Brothers Islands
19. Port Ghalib/Marsa Alam
20. Sha'ab Samadai
21. Elphinstone Reef
22. Daedalus Reef
23. Hamata and Fury Shoals
24. Zabargad and Rocky Island
25. St John's Reef

Taba

- Dive type: Reef
- Ability level: Beginner to experienced
- Depth: 6–30 m (20–100 ft)
- Snorkelling: yes
- Rating: ★★★

Sea Moths are just one of the weirder fish species found at Taba.

Adjacent to Israel, the Egyptian town of Taba grew up as the international border between the two countries. It now boasts a few upmarket resorts for those who want to take advantage of both countries. However, the diving claim to fame here is for some of the weird and wonderful critters that can be found on the sandy plain before it slopes steeply down into the depths of the north-western Red Sea.

There are around 20 individual dive sites along this short stretch of coastline and whilst the road crosses an international border, the sea has no such boundaries so that Israeli dive boats cross into Egypt and vice-versa.

The most famous of the sites is Moses Rock, a large coral outcrop with a few smaller ones nearby. Close to the edge of the drop-off, this large coral rock is a microcosm of marine life in an otherwise featureless plain. However, at night the seabed comes alive with small molluscs, burrowing starfish, anemones, tube worms, curious fish-like stargazers and the Sea Moth. The latter is just as at home in Indonesia and walks along the seabed on adapted

pelvic fins. With its curious long snout it feeds on tiny crustaceans. Moses Rock also has the most common endemic fish, the Red Sea Anemonefish.

Maxwell's Reef is a rare find offshore, which usually has eagle rays and simply 'clouds' of the ubiquitous anthias goldfish. I first dived the Fjord over 35 years ago, which is essentially a deep basin, bay or marsa. The sandy seabed is dotted with small coral boulders where stonefish, blue-spotted rays and small moray eels are found. The Canyon is usually on most photographers' lists because it boasts rare frogfish, usually found in more tropical waters.

The Fjord is a natural inlet to the south of Taba.

Coral Island

- Dive type: Reef
- Ability level: Beginner to experienced
- Depth: 12–25 m (40–80 ft)
- Snorkelling: yes
- Rating: ★★★

Long-nosed Hawkfish are found on most seafans.

Coral Island or Pharaoh's Island is also in the Taba region and is now under Egyptian control, largely rebuilt over the years according to their idea of what the island looked like. There is a superb drawing of the island, originally called the Isle of Graia, by David Roberts in 1839. When I first visited Coral Island back in 1974, the old walls of the ancient fortress were in ruin. Located 11 km (6¾ miles) south of Eilat, the original Muslim fortress was first built by Saladin in 1170 and was reputed to have housed the Queen of Sheba. It had a port at one time that is now silted up. Archaeological works have uncovered artefacts from Byzantium and Roman times, much of which was underwater.

The eastern side of the island facing into the Gulf of Aqaba/Eilat is the most interesting as it is a steeply sloping wall of the fringing reef that tumbles down into the depths. Large stony corals predominate and the usual anthias, chromis, Sergeant Majors, fusiliers, wrasses and jacks are always around. At around 25 m (82 ft) there a few large gorgonian seafans, which usually yield another of those Red Sea rarities: the Long-nose

Hawkfish. I call this species the 'tartan' fish as its pale body is crossed with both horizontal and vertical stripes. The smaller coral recesses have small groups of Glassy Sweepers and Hatchetfish, predated upon by at least two species of lionfish.

The inside edge of the island is quite sandy, interspersed with small coral heads where Blue-spotted Stingrays are quite common. At night, small molluscs inhabit this sea floor, and there are always burrowing starfish and worms to be found. Crocodile fish appear quite common around here and you should see them regularly.

David Roberts' iconic lithograph of Coral Island.

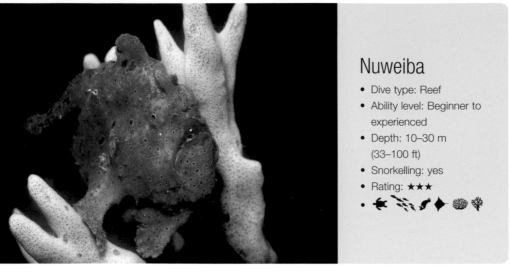

Nuweiba

- Dive type: Reef
- Ability level: Beginner to experienced
- Depth: 10–30 m (33–100 ft)
- Snorkelling: yes
- Rating: ★★★

Frogfish are actually quite common – if you can find them!

Still associated with local Bedouin encampments and named after the Bedouin 'Bubbling Springs', Nuweiba has long been a favourite site for people on a dive safari. It's located 80 km (50 miles) south of Eilat and 185 km (115 miles) north of Sharm el-Sheikh. Nuweiba is only recently becoming more developed by the larger hotel chains, previously it was a favourite place for backpackers. Entry is always from the shore. I first dived these steep reefs at the edge of an even steeper sand slope in 1974 and was astonished at the variety of marine life to be found so close to the shore. South Cove to the north and Tarabin (Terabien) Beach are very popular with both divers and snorkellers, and the site has risen in popularity with divers and underwater photographers as the Egyptian centre for macro and muck diving.

More than 50 species of nudibranch have been found here, but what is particularly special are at least two species of ghost pipefish, a Sea Moth, a handful of different frogfish, fire gobies, burrowing sand gobies and their resident shrimps, and the quite large population of Green Turtles, which feeds on the seagrass beds found all along this 16-km (10-mile) stretch of coastline.

It is rare to have encounters with sharks or rays, but the little critters more than make up for the lack of big species. Nuweiba has two marine parks: Ras Mamlach and Ras Abu Galum with superb, steep walls and drop-offs, but there will be a fee to be paid for these dive sites. Other diving can be found at Res el-Burqa and the Coral Gardens, which always have plenty of lionfish, clownfish and moray eels.

Nudibranchs or sea slugs come in many exotic colours.

Ras Abu Galum

- Dive type: Reef
- Ability level: Beginner to experienced
- Depth: 1–30 m (3–100 ft)
- Snorkelling: yes
- Rating: ★★★

Often swept by currents these reefs are rarely dived.

This marine preserve located north of Dahab used to be reached only by camel along the narrow coastal strip running north from Nuweiba. Subsequently, this journey was undertaken by four-wheel-drive as the fringing reef is almost directly next to the shore. We used to always dive at the 'named' sites, yet the entire coastline is simply phenomenal. You could stop and dive literally anywhere and fully expect to experience all of the general Red Sea marine life on offer.

Our early days of Red Sea exploration utilized all of the above in the quest to rediscover forgotten dive sites and discover new and exciting dive experiences. My memories (aided by my logbook musings) describe the reef here as mixed between steeply sloping and near vertical walls interspersed with numerous sand chutes. I remember some parts that looked like they may have belonged to an ancient shipwreck, but the overwhelming feeling was of pristine reefs, great soft and hard corals and a very obvious zonation at around 25 m (80 ft) where the large gorgonian sea fans were found. Sergeant Majors, chromis, anthias, yellow goatfish and even huge pufferfish can be found here and the water column usually has barracuda, unicornfish and emperorfish.

There are many small clams on the reef crests and large anemones with their symbiotic Clownfish, but also in this mix are Three-spot Dascyllus, a few small shrimps and even a couple of species of crab, which also enjoy the protection of the anemone's stinging tentacles. A steep sand slope drops into the depths and if you dive to the left (north), the reef curves out from the shore and becomes more vertical. Always keep your eyes out into the blue for large pelagics and turtles.

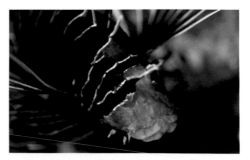

Lionfish are found in many of the overhanging coral boulders.

Dahab

- Dive type: Reef
- Ability Level: Beginner to experienced & technical
- Depth: 1– >100 m (3– >330 ft)
- Snorkelling: yes
- Rating: ★★★★★

The Blue Hole arch starts at 56 m (190 ft).

Dahab has a huge number and variety of dive sites to suit everyone from the complete beginner to the most experienced of technical divers. The Blue Hole is a geological formation that is not a true blue hole; rather it has been formed by the influx of fresh mountain water, which inhibited coral growth and created a large feature that curves out from the rather straight coastline reef. The arch starts at 56 m (190 ft) and the bottom is way below at 120 m (400 ft). The hole itself is awe-inspiring, but the coral growth along the outer edge of the fringing reef is absolutely spectacular, unlike the growth inside the pool area, which is quite barren.

Whilst most divers just enter the Blue Hole pool off the rocky shoreline, an alternative entry is to take a short walk to the north side of the hole where divers (one at a time) can enter a chimney on the reef crest and exit at around 30 m (100 ft). This is not a dive to be taken lightly and for the last few years the Blue Hole has become one of the main locations for mixed gas and rebreather diving.

Nearby and south of the Blue Hole is the Canyon, a crevasse that cuts down through the steeply sloping coral reef. There are only a couple of exits. These are quite deep, so once committed to diving through the canyon, you really have to go all the way down to around 50 m (170 ft); the reef does drop down to 100 m (328 ft) and this is a regular haunt for technical divers.

Although this is a shore dive, Sinai Divers often visit with their live-aboard dive boat.

The Gardens

- Dive type: Reef
- Ability level: Beginner to experienced
- Depth: 6–25 m (20–70 ft)
- Snorkelling: yes
- Rating: ★★★

Ornate Ghost Pipefish are on everyone's wishlist.

Further south and just outside Na'ama Bay can be found the Gardens (Near, Middle and Far Garden). At the northern entrance to the bay, these sites are primarily used for trainee dives, for snorkelling and for night dives as you do not have to go far from the bay and have everything close to hand.

My great friend Bob Johnson found me my first Ornate Ghost Pipefish here back in 1983. These very rare fish are more commonly associated with the tropical reefs of Indonesia, so to find them in the northern Red Sea is amazing. The three Garden dives all have fairly steeply sloping reefs interspersed with small coral heads, various swimthroughs and sand chutes. There is a lot of coral rubble. Do not be disappointed by the lack of big schools of fish, as the little critters more than make up for them. There are some amazing small species to see here, especially Spanish Dancers and Lanternfish, which have a bio-luminescent patch under each eye that can be turned off and on by an opaque black membrane. At only 12 cm (5 in) long, they are never seen during daylight hours and are usually only found

below 7 m (23 ft). There are good lettuce corals, leathery corals, scorpionfish, clownfish, lionfish and anthias.

Curiously, because the headland to the bay juts out into the tidal stream, divers regularly see larger pelagic fish out in the blue, such as Whale Sharks and eagle rays.

Spanish Dancer (*Hexabranchus sanguineus*)

The Tower

- Dive type: Reef wall
- Ability level: Beginner to experienced
- Depth: 5–45 m (17–150 ft)
- Snorkelling: yes
- Rating: ★★★★
- 🐬 🐟 🪸 🌿

The tower has vertical walls covered in all manner of invertebrates.

The Tower is midway between Na'ama Bay and Ras Umm Sid. It's a shore dive and very close to the United Nations MFO base, so can be accessed by jeep and a fairly rough scramble over the ancient beach rock, then a drop into a small natural amphitheatre and down into the depths. At around 5 m (17 ft) there is a crevice in the coral and you can drop inside this and exit further down the wall. The old coral walls are largely underhanging, providing numerous recesses and crevices in which to discover interesting fish and invertebrates. The Tower is basically an outcrop from the shore that can be seen from the sea and is located to the south of the entrance.

Night diving here is simply out of this world. The more vertical southern side has excellent soft corals as it is in much more natural light and these corals host various small shrimps, squat lobsters, crinoids, basket stars and sleeping fish. Spanish Dancer nudibranchs are also known to be found here regularly and, as this is an under-dived location, the marine life is excellent and the corals in good condition.

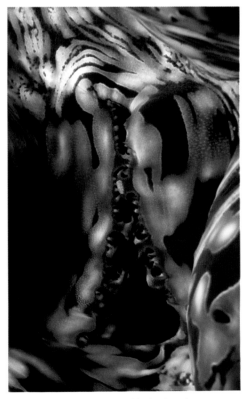

Clams are found amidst many of the hard corals.

Ras Umm Sid

- Dive type: Reef wall
- Ability level: Beginner to experienced
- Depth: 30 cm–45 m (1–150 ft)
- Snorkelling: yes
- Rating: ★★★★

Giant seafans are found near the corner at Ras Umm Sid.

Ras Umm Sid is the first headland before you turn north when leaving the twin harbours at Sharm el-Sheikh and Sharm el-Moiya. Often done as a boat dive, the shore dive at the headland is astonishing to say the least. There is a very shallow reef crest platform only 30 cm (1 ft) deep, which you can stroll over until you get to the first of the holes. Sitting on the edge of the hole in the reef crest where fish are swimming below is enough enticement for you to just roll into the water and follow a winding gallery of ancient coral forms until you appear at the edge of the vertical wall around 6 m (20 ft) deep. As you swim down the reef, exploring the various caves and caverns, you come to a huge gorgonian sea fan forest towards the corner at around 25 m (80 ft). Here there are Long-nose Hawkfish and Axillary Wrasse, as well as Emperor Angelfish, squirrelfish and tons of Glassy Sweepers. The site gets very busy as you can imagine, but if you get here first thing as the sun is coming up, the reef just lights up and sparkles in the early morning light. I love it

Frogfish are often found at this site.

Ras Umm Sid has a resident population of large batfish.

Straits of Tiran

Gordon Reef

- Dive type: Reef wall & wreck
- Ability level: Beginner to experienced
- Depth: 30 cm– >45 m (1– >150 ft)
- Snorkelling: yes
- Rating: ★★★★★

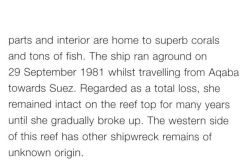

The reefs here are not as steeply sloping.

The dive sites in the Straits of Tiran are clustered around four separate reefs in the midst of the channel between the Sinai mainland and Tiran Island (Gordon, Thomas, Woodhouse and Jackson Reefs); each of them is distinct and all of them are well worth diving. The reefs are located just to the west of Tiran Island and whilst the channel between Tiran and the reefs is very deep, virtually all of the commercial shipping traffic passes to the west of the reefs.

The most southerly is Gordon Reef, which is slightly horseshoe-shaped with an unknown wreck to its western side, plus the shipwreck *Loullia* on its northern edge. Gordon Reef has a wide, shallow, sandy platform where most dive boats anchor, either for the day, or to stay overnight and allow guests to have a night dive. The small coral boulders that dot the sandy area are little oases of marine life. The remains of the 2,479-ton *Loullia* are well worth exploring when the currents are in your favour and now that the wreck is completely open, the stranded

parts and interior are home to superb corals and tons of fish. The ship ran aground on 29 September 1981 whilst travelling from Aqaba towards Suez. Regarded as a total loss, she remained intact on the reef top for many years until she gradually broke up. The western side of this reef has other shipwreck remains of unknown origin.

The wreck of the *Loullia* is disintegrating rapidly.

Thomas Reef

- Dive type: Reef wall
- Ability level: Beginner to experienced
- Depth: 30 cm– >45 m (1– >150 ft)
- Snorkelling: yes
- Rating: ★★★★★

The southern corner of Thomas is rarely dived and then only from a live-aboard boat.

Travelling north, Thomas Reef is next which, with favourable currents, can be circumnavigated in one dive. It is fairly circular in shape and is rarely dived, as most of the day dive boats from Sharm and Na'ama Bay go directly to the south-eastern tip of Jackson Reef. However, Thomas Reef has a stunning, steeply sloping wall to the west. There are a few small caverns where white-tip sharks can be found 'sleeping' during daylight hours and the reef crest is simply alive with many species of parrotfish and wrasse, chromis and Sergeant Majors.

Large table corals are found next to the far corner of the reef.

The southern corner of Thomas is rarely dived and then only from a live-aboard.

Straits of Tiran

Woodhouse Reef

- Dive type: Reef wall
- Ability level: Beginner to experienced
- Depth: 30 cm– >45 m (1– >150 ft)
- Snorkelling: yes
- Rating: ★★★★★
-

The four reefs in the Straits of Tiran are on everyone's dive list.

Further on north is the long, cigar-shaped Woodhouse Reef, aligned in a north-south direction, with its northern edge reached from Jackson Reef across the saddle that joins the two reefs. This reef is near vertical for the first 18 m (60 ft), then slopes steeply with the eastern face dropping into a massive chasm. Again, few divers ever do this dive as there are no moorings and dive-boat crews have to work to keep an eye on their charges. Yet the dive is spectacular with great schools of fish and superb encounters with turtles. Hammerhead Sharks may be seen at dawn or dusk.

The crest on Thomas Reef is covered in healthy corals.

Jackson Reef

- Dive type: Reef wall & wreck
- Ability level: Beginner to experienced
- Depth: 30 cm– >45 m (1– >150 ft)
- Snorkelling: yes
- Rating: ★★★★★

Schools of fish sweep past these reefs.

The northernmost reef is Jackson Reef. Elliptical in shape, it has the remains of the shipwreck *Lara* on its north-western corner and virtually every dive boat anchors on its south-eastern corner due to the northerly prevailing winds. Once dominated by the wreck of the *Lara*, which ran aground on 11 September 1982, now only the bare skeleton can be seen. The entire ship has broken apart, been partly salvaged or has dropped over into the depths, with the main debris field starting at around 40 m (134 ft). The reef itself is spectacular and even though it is one of the most popular day-boat dive sites, it remains remarkably pristine, testimony to the richness of the marine life in this region. Thankfully the snorkel boats are not allowed to anchor on the reef anymore, leaving much more room for everyone. During the winter months hammerhead sharks are known to patrol the north-west corner and there is a small cavern with 'sleeping' Whitetip Reef Sharks near the north-east corner. When conditions are perfect, you are able to traverse the saddle between Jackson Reef and Woodhouse Reef with fairly good chances of seeing large pelagics.

The remains of the *Lara* can still be found on Jackson Reef.

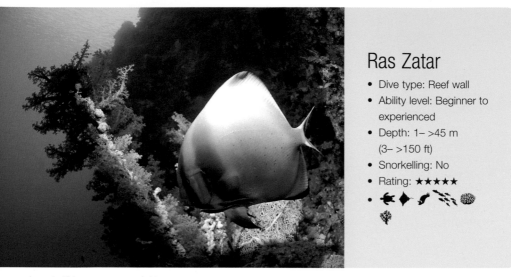

Ras Zatar

- Dive type: Reef wall
- Ability level: Beginner to experienced
- Depth: 1– >45 m (3– >150 ft)
- Snorkelling: No
- Rating: ★★★★★
- 🐢 ◆ 🐟 🐟 🪸 🪸

Large batfish are a common sight.

The southernmost point before you enter into the huge bay known as Marsa Bareika is an absolutely spectacular dive, but best done only in the morning due to the position of the sun. The dive is unpopular with many day-boat captains, as there are no moorings here and dive staff have to remain vigilant when there are divers in the water. The reef wall is very steeply sloping when you enter and, since the prevailing current here is northwards, it will gently push you along towards the corner, where the wall becomes deeply indented, vertical and even overhanging in many places. In the shallows, huge caverns have been carved out by tidal action and geological activity, and it is here that there are staggering numbers of Glassy Sweepers. Around the edges of these schools can be found hundreds of lionfish, soldierfish and even large groupers, all waiting to strike at the ever-moving shoals of fish. Transient tuna will also swoop into the shoals here and you can often see turtles or even mantas and Whale Sharks out in the blue.

Ras Zatar is one of my top Red Sea dive sites.

Lionfish lie in wait for passing Glassy Sweepers.

Ras Muhammad

- Dive type: Reef wall & wreck
- Ability level: Beginner to experienced
- Depth: 1– >100 m (3– >330 ft)
- Snorkelling: yes
- Rating: ★★★★★

Ras Muhammad is the Number One dive site in the Red Sea.

The tip of the Sinai Peninsula is probably one of the most famous dive sites in the world, and quite rightly so. There are vertical walls plummeting from the surface into the depths, massive schools of fish, gardens of anemones with their clownfish and damselfish partners, sharks, rays, turtles, shipwreck remains and simply thousands of anthias – the quintessential view of the entire Red Sea. There are three submarine sea mounts or ergs here, connected by a shallow saddle of coral rubble, small coral heads and to the south-west, the remains of the shipwreck *Jolanda*.

The *Jolanda* struck the reef on 1 April 1980 on her way from Piraeus to Aqaba during rough weather and wedged herself between the ergs. Her cargo of small containers filled with pet food, toilets, sinks, pipework and even a BMW car all spilled out onto the shallower part of the reef saddle. She finally succumbed to nature and plummeted into the depths in the summer of 1985. Technical divers can find her at approximately 160 m (530 ft)!

Dives at Ras Muhammed usually start near the Anemone Gardens (Anemone City) just off the last point of the mainland. Divers then traverse the drop-off towards Shark Reef where the current picks up and carries them around to the saddle. If you have plenty of air left (not having spent it in the depths hunting sharks), the current will take you to Jolanda (Yolanda) Reef where you are swept around at approximately 9 m (30 ft) to an easily negotiated cavern, with lots of Glassy Sweepers, and wire corals and their associated Whip Coral Gobies and Shrimps. The remains of your air are usually spent hovering over the shipwreck detritus before being picked up by the dive-boat's tender. Shark Reef is renowned for huge schools of batfish, barracuda, emperorfish, jacks and unicornfish all year round, but during July to September the numbers increase a hundredfold.

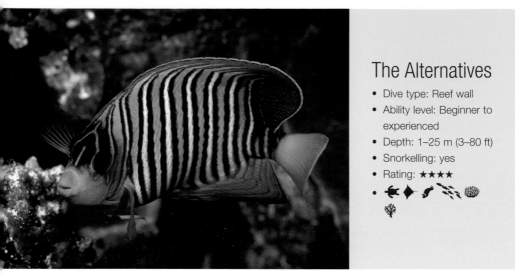

The Alternatives

- Dive type: Reef wall
- Ability level: Beginner to experienced
- Depth: 1–25 m (3–80 ft)
- Snorkelling: yes
- Rating: ★★★★
-

Regal Angelfish are commonly seen.

Now recognised in their own right, the Alternatives were so named as the 'alternative' site to dive when Ras Muhammad was blown out by bad weather or when the currents were too strong to dive safely. Along the south-western coast of the Sinai Peninsula, a low string of coral ergs run perpendicular to the shore on the way up to Sha'ab Ali in the eastern Gulf of Suez. These coral heads are perfect protection as a safe anchorage for the live-aboard dive boats and each reef can be attached by line giving a reference point to return to the dive boat safely. The outer mini wall is host to very good soft corals, gorgonian sea fans and simply tons of interesting invertebrates all of which vie for your attention at night. The saddles between each erg always have a few different species of moray eel and the outer reef is patrolled by small schools of tuna. Blue-spotted Stingrays are found under most coral ledges, as are crocodilefish and scorpionfish.

Pristine soft corals cover these reefs.

Anthias goldfish are the most common of all fish in the Red Sea.

Sha'ab Ali

- Dive type: Reef wall & wrecks
- Ability level: Beginner to experienced
- Depth: 15–30 m (50–100 ft)
- Snorkelling: No (except with dolphins)
- Rating: ★★★★★

The *Thistlegorm* is very popular with all divers.

Sha'ab Ali is a massive, shallow, coral-reef system that juts out into the Gulf of Suez along the south-western coast of the Sinai. There are numerous reefs, isolated lagoons, hidden sandbars, deep channels and wrecks of ships that either ventured up the wrong passage like the *Dunraven*, or, like the *Thistlegorm* and the *Rosalie Moller* in the western approaches, were bombed at anchor.

The *Dunraven* carrying general cargo struck the reef near Beacon Rock on 25 April 1876 on her way to the Suez Canal. Currents are quite strong at this exposed corner of Sha'ab Ali and divers should expect to dive to 30 m (100 ft) to get the full experience of this 80-m (262-ft) long ship. By far the most famous of all the Red Sea shipwrecks is the *Thistlegorm*. Built in 1940 in Sunderland, she finally met her demise on 6 October 1941 when she was bombed whilst at anchor in Sha'ab Ali. Thankfully you can spend virtually the entire dive within the ship's cavernous holds exploring and recognising, trucks, motorbikes, railway trains, guns and just about everything else in between. Her bow is virtually

free from marine life (only due to the succession of mooring buoys that have been placed there) and is found in only 15 m (50 ft) of water. Directly behind are various winches, etc., before you reach the first of the holds. Dropping down inside is akin to a freefall into a military museum with armaments and artefacts all around you and, once comfortable with your depth and your dive lights switched on, you can enjoy one of the most amazing dive experiences of your life. In between dives on the *Thistlegorm*, guests get the chance to explore one of the nearby sheltered lagoons, where a party of Bottlenose Dolphins have a permanent home and appear to really enjoy the interaction with us ungainly swimmers.

Whilst not in Sha'ab Ali, but over to the west off Gubal, the *Rosalie Moller* was bombed shortly after the *Thistlegorm* and now lies in 18–40 m (60–131 ft) of water. There is the possibility of seeing an Ornate Ghost Pipefish here. The live-aboard usually arrives in the late afternoon, once all the day boats leave. This allows a less-crowded dive time in the afternoon, then a night dive and an early morning dive before breakfast.

Shag Rock

- Dive type: Reef & wreck
- Ability level: Beginner to experienced
- Depth: 6–18 m (20–60 ft)
- Snorkelling: yes
- Rating: ★★★★★
-

The stern of the *Kingston* is very photogenic.

Roughly shaped like an upside-down teardrop, Shag Rock is named after the large population of shags, which sit on the small coral outcrops to dry their wings, testimony to the abundant fish life found around the reef. Usually when boats anchor here overnight, they will hang off the bottom point as the prevailing winds are generally from the north and the currents also sweep down each side of the reef, keeping a dive boat in place. However, most boats just travel to the north-west corner where the remains of the *Kingston*, which ploughed into the reef on 22 February 1881, can be found. Her forequarters were completely destroyed, but her boilers are still evident and now her stern sits on the seabed at 18 m (60 ft). The reef structure has grown out over the wreck making her one of the most photogenic of all the Red Sea wrecks. Her aft decks have rotted away revealing the iron superstructure. You can descend some way inside the ship and traverse her interior. Coal from her boilers is quite evident and the scene looking upwards to the surface is just superb. Her stern is covered in small tubastrea corals, which glow to a brilliant golden colour at night. Schools of surgeonfish, Glassy

Sweepers, groupers, tiny shrimps, anemones with clownfish – in fact, all of the creatures that you would expect to see on a very healthy reef are found here on the wreck.

If you aren't sufficiently enticed by the wreck to hang around, allow the current to take you to the south, where you will find a huge propeller from another long-lost ship and some superbly shaped spiral formations of table coral. Dolphins' 'clicks' are constantly heard in the waters around you and quite often they will buzz you as they swim by. A fantastic wreck dive.

Shag Rock is a photographer's paradise.

Sha'ab Abu Nuhas

- Dive type: Sloping Reef & wrecks
- Ability level: Beginner to experienced
- Depth: 3–25 m (10–80 ft)
- Snorkelling: yes
- Rating: ★★★★★

Masked Butterflyfish congregate in large numbers.

Of all the small reefs in all the world, Sha'ab Abu Nuhas has to score very high for shipwreck exploration as there are four wrecks along her north shore.

On 22 April 1983, whilst living in the Red Sea and working on board the *Lady Jenny III*, we intercepted a may-day distress signal from a freighter that had struck a reef to the north of Shadwan Island. The sea was ferocious and we were unable to get close enough to help. This was the *Giannis D*. Fortunately her crew escaped unhurt. A year to the day after she sank we had our first anniversary dive, now that the ship was completely underwater. The bows were sheared off, the hold all but collapsed, but the stern section, engine room and bridge were all virtually intact and lying at 45 degrees to port at the bottom of the reef in 10–28 m (33–94 ft) of water. Her bent propeller is partly buried in the sand, but perhaps the best aspect of the dive is to explore the engine room, which is filled with Glassy Sweepers and lionfish. The entire superstructure is now covered in hard and soft corals, small sponges, clams and everything else in between.

A year later, a team of us decided to swim east along the north shore of Abu Nuhas. Adrian O'Neil, Captain of the *Lady Jenny V*, was the lead diver, so he is credited with first finding the remains of an ancient shipwreck. Some months later, it was confirmed by the P&O (the Peninsular and Oriental Steamship Company) that this ship was the SS *Carnatic*, lost on 13 September 1869. The author is credited with discovering the ship's identity. She carried a valuable cargo of specie (unstamped coin of the realm) that was all salvaged along with copper sheets and ingots. Completely encrusted in coral growth with her deck planks long since rotted away, you can see clearly into her interior. Schools of Glassy Sweepers are everywhere.

Further to the east are another two massive shipwrecks: the *Chrisoula K* and the *Kimon M*. There has been some controversy over the years as to the number of shipwrecks on this exposed reef. It is confirmed that there are only four wrecks and all of them are superb dive sites. The diving here is subject to good sea conditions as the north-facing reef is quite exposed.

El Gouna Hurghada

- Dive type: Reef & wreck
- Ability level: Beginner to experienced
- Depth: 6– >45m (20– >50ft)
- Snorkelling: yes
- Rating: ★★★★★

Huge Lettuce Corals predominate on this reef.

Hurghada has been developed as a tourist destination in its own right; El Gouna, 20 km (12½ miles) to the north, is recognised as a staging post for exploring all of the western Red Sea reefs. From here day dive boats are able to access the wrecks on Sha'ab Abu Nuhas, Carless reef, Umm Qamar Island and Reef, Siyul Kebira, Blind Reef, Sha'ab El Erg and a few others.

Siyul Kebira is a small island around 30 minutes' north of El Gouna and is surrounded by a fringing reef with two dive sites, one at the north-eastern corner and the other known as El Gilwa at the southern side of the island. Both have an abundance of marine life and you should expect to see moray eels, turtles, schools of glassfish amongst the coral pinnacles, plenty of lionfish and sometimes Leopard Sharks on the sand and coral rubble seabed.

Directly east of El Gouna is Sha'ab El Erg, which is a horseshoe-shaped reef where the lagoon is home to a number of Bottlenose Dolphins. Snorkellers often make this trip for the fair chance of a good interaction with them. Known as Dolphin House, the reef to each side of the lagoon is very good and there are usually scorpionfish, crocodilefish and plenty of lionfish, all after the schools of anthias and Glassy Sweepers. There is even a Manta Point here, as in so many other locations in the world, but the mantas themselves are few and far between.

The rare Citron Goby is found in large numbers.

Brothers Islands

- Dive type: Reef wall & wreck
- Ability level: Beginner to experienced
- Depth: 1– >60 m (3– >200 ft)
- Snorkelling: yes
- Rating: *★★★★★
-

The lighthouse on Big Brother Island.

Some 200 km (124 miles) south of Ras Muhammed and 65 km (40 miles) east of El Qusier are the Brothers Islands, part of Egypt's National Parks since 1983 and known locally as El Akhawein. These two ancient volcanic peaks topped with limestone caps are just 1 km (⅔ mile) apart with Big Brother to the north and Little Brother to the south. Big Brother is topped with an operational lighthouse, first built by the British in 1883.

There are two shipwrecks to the north of Big Brother: the *Numidia*, which struck the reef and sank on only her second voyage on 19 July 1901, and to the south-west of her, the *Aida*, which was damaged during the same raids that sunk the *Thistlegorm* and the *Rosalie Moller* in October 1941. After the raid, which only slightly damaged the *Aida*, the Captain ran her aground, in case of further attacks. She was then refloated and repaired and continued her service until 15 September 1957 when she struck the island during heavy seas. She now lies from 25–60 m (80–200 ft) and is just one more reason to dive these amazing islands.

Virtually all of the *Numidia*'s 7,000 tons of cargo were salvaged but parts of her two railway engines are still in the shallows. Most divers start on the *Numidia* and can explore the ship at their leisure before continuing with the north-to-south prevailing current. The east flank is dived in the morning and the west in the afternoon.

The diving at the Brothers Islands is as good as it gets in the Red Sea and certainly knocks spots off the northern reefs which have seen so much diver damage. With very little dive-boat traffic, the reefs and walls are pristine. On Big Brother there are Thresher Sharks (identified by their distinctive long tails), Grey Reef Sharks and even Oceanic Whitetip Sharks, turtles, barracudas and massive shoals of jacks. The gorgonian seafans and large black coral trees can be found as shallow as five metres (17 ft) and as always, the reef crest is smothered in golden anthias, which just light up the sea around you. Just off Little Brother, part of our group snorkelled with dolphins, and dived with Whitetip Reef Sharks and several turtles. For those who are more technically qualifed, there is a deep dive to the plateau south of Little Brother.

Port Ghalib/
Marsa Alam

- Dive type: Reef wall & wreck
- Ability level: Beginner to experienced
- Depth: 1– >45 m (3– >150 ft)
- Snorkelling: yes
- Rating: ★★★★
- 🐢 ◆ 🐟 🐠 🪸 🪸

Chromis are shy fish and hide in the corals when you approach.

Whilst this region is always advertised as Marsa Alam, the tourist area and airport is actually Port Ghalib. It is the port for many of the dive boats, which frequent these reefs. Marsa Alam to the south is still a small Bedouin fishing village but most of the larger live-aboards are accessed from the bay here for travelling further south.

One of the farther reefs visited by the day-boats is Marsa Morena. The northern aspect of this large bay is dotted with big coral ergs or bommies, which obviously attract all manner of fish life. The northern corner plateau is more diffuse with smaller soft and hard corals, but it is the coral heads leading into the bay that are superb. One, in particular, has a massive table coral and there are always a couple of Masked Butterflyfish and a Coral Grouper hiding underneath. Large scorpionfish are found on every dive, as are Crocodile Fish and lionfish. Curiously, as these bays are only fringed with corals, the sandy regions attract huge stingrays, guitar sharks, turtles, tuna and a number of other large pelagics that are often considered rare in other regions of the Red Sea.

Most of the bays have a scattering of seagrass, some more than others, and it is here that you can find large Green and Hawksbill Turtles feeding or resting, usually with their attendant remora suckerfish.

Closer towards Port Ghalib is Marsa Souni Kebir, one of only a few bays left where there is no commercial development. The fringing reef to the south of the bay is superb with several sightings of turtle, large schools of Circular Spadefish, schools of Bigeye, squirrelfish, goatfish and Longspot Snapper all mixed together.

This is one of the few sites where Dugong are found regularly.

Sha'ab Samadai (Dolphin Reef)

- Dive type: Reef lagoon, coral pinnacles
- Ability level: Beginner to experienced
- Depth: 3–30 m (10–100 ft)
- Snorkelling: yes
- Rating: ★★★★★

The shallow caverns on this reef are safe and easy to dive.

As Sha'ab Samadai is part of Egypt's Marine Parks, all visiting boats have to be accompanied by a Marine Park Ranger and all divers are briefed on the strict conservation policies enforced. This horseshoe-shaped reef is not only home to a family of Spinner Dolphins, but the reef pinnacles are also famous for their easily negotiated caverns and swimthroughs. Day-boats always leave from Marsa Alam to moor off the north-western corner, with easy access to the coral pinnacles, all of which are packed with some of the rarest critters I have found in the Red Sea, including the Robust Ghost Pipefish. With an average depth of only 12–25 m (40–82 ft), the visibility is so good that you can clearly see each of the narrow, vertical coral heads making navigation simple and the diving exceptional. The largest of the reefs has a massive open cavern system, which is easily negotiable in only 6 m (20 ft) of water with numerous exits and open shafts of light everywhere. Large sweetlips and emperorfish inhabit this reef and all are very friendly.

This is a great dive with vertical walls covered in soft and hard corals, schools of anthias, and perhaps even a Whitetip Reef Shark. The sandy gullies between the coral heads have a number of large anemones and anemonefish and the small patches of seagrass host sea horses, frogfish and Sea Moths. It is absolutely amazing that such a wide variety of rare species could be found in such a small area.

The outer reef ergs are covered in soft corals.

Elphinstone Reef

- Dive type: Reef wall
- Ability level: Beginner to experienced
- Depth: 1– >60 m (3– >200 ft)
- Snorkelling: yes
- Rating: ★★★★★
-

The wall at Elphinstone is simply superb.

Elphinstone Reef is 2½ hours' boat ride from Marsa Alam, but less so from Hamata. This long, finger-thin reef running in a north–south direction comes to just below the surface. There is usually a surface surge, swell and current that tends to run in a north–south direction, so divers are briefed meticulously on how to negotiate the reef and on correct exit and entry procedures from the boat. The first dive in the morning is south along the eastern flank with the near vertical wall on the right that is simply covered in very colourful soft corals and the ubiquitous anthias. If you are happy to concentrate on the vertical reef walls, you may well be honoured with large schools of jacks, spadefish, tuna, mackerel and barracudas. The shallower sections of the reef, whilst disturbed by the oceanic swell, have superb shoals of snapper, Raccoon Butterflyfish and pufferfish. The western flank is not as vertical, but in many places there are small fissures and caverns with simply tons of fish. Sadly there is no night diving here due to its isolated location.

Divers enjoy the brilliant soft corals.

Bannerfish are common in shallow water.

Daedalus Reef

- Dive type: Reef wall
- Ability level: Beginner to experienced
- Depth: 3– >30 m (10– >100 ft)
- Snorkelling: yes
- Rating: ★★★★★

Daedalus is on the live-aboard's itinerary.

Also known as Abu Kizan (the name comes from an old shipwreck which sank at the north-western corner carrying a cargo of pottery. 'Kizan' is Arabic for 'pottery'), Daedalus is usually accessed from both Port Ghalib and Marsa Alam by the long-range, live-aboard dive boats, but now day-boats are also running to this offshore reef from Hamata. Topped with another of the Red Sea lighthouses, this was built in 1863 and rebuilt in 1931. At 30 m (100 ft) tall, the lighthouse is still active and also houses the Egyptian Navy and Coastguard in an adjacent two-storey blockhouse. The lighthouse sits on an artificial island on top of a beautiful, shallow coral reef, which is around 400 m (1,310 ft) long by 100 m (330 ft) at its widest part. Known for the regular encounters with hammerhead sharks and many other large pelagic fish, often in their thousands, Daedalus has been at the top of divers' wishlist for many years.

Currents are similar here to Elphinstone and run in a north–south direction. Being so far offshore, it can get very windy, making the surface conditions somewhat challenging. Corals are superb here with large black coral trees and huge gorgonians, as well as tons of basslets, chromis and damselfish. There are always large schools of jacks, barracudas, emperorfish and unicornfish. The maximum depth for your second dive should not be deeper than your first, as this may entail long safety stops where you may be able to enjoy more sharks!

Vertical walls are synonymous of this reef.

Hamata and the Fury Shoals

- Dive type: Reef, wrecks
- Ability level: Beginner to experienced
- Depth: 1– >30 m (3– >100 ft)
- Snorkelling: yes
- Rating: ★★★★★

Lionfish are a common sight.

Hamata has only one small dive resort that is like stepping back in time and is located around two hour's drive south of Port Ghalib. The Emperor Divers resort is used as a staging post to dive Fury Shoals and Rocky Island on a daily dive-boat basis, as well as for exploring the local reefs, without the need for a live-aboard dive boat. Sataya to the south of Fury Shoals is only two hour's boat ride away.

The house reef at Hamata is easily accessed along a new pier and is perfect for underwater photographers who can spend lots of time in shallow water exploring the nooks and crannies of the reef to see cuttlefish, lizardfish and even stargazers. There are a number of offshore reefs with the furthest north being the Qula'an Islands. Fantastic for macro life, you can also have great sightings of eagle rays and even a few Whitetip Reef Sharks. At depths of under 15 m (50 ft) they are perfect for exploring as a third or fourth dive of the day.

Abu Galawa Soraya has the wreckage of a small sailing boat in 18 m (60 ft) of water, which is still intact and virtually covered in fire coral and small stony corals. Sha'ab Claudio is always on

Dolphins are the main attraction here.

the live-aboard's deep south exploration list as it is an easy dive and a superb shallow cavern system with numerous entrances and exits, and completely open in aspect to allow for safe and shallow exploration whilst you hunt for critters.

Abu Galawa Kebir is popular as an overnight mooring for live-aboards and is host to the *Tien Hsing* Chinese tugboat, which is simply superb as a dive site, and is surrounded by coral-smothered vertical walls and pinnacles typical of the Fury Shoals.

Sha'ab Ruhr is a huge reef close to Hamata dive shop that offers great protection for diving in all weather and sea conditions. The eastern reef slopes steeply down to 20 m (67 ft) and has a huge coral mountain just attached to the reef. The western reef has many smaller pinnacles and there are simply hundreds of species of fish

schooling here, as well as some great macro critter hunting.

Sha'ab Mohammed is a series of pinnacles, which also can only be dived in calm water conditions. Often done as a drift dive, Spinner Dolphins and sharks can be seen here, as the main dolphin lagoon is located to the south of this offshore reef. Sataya is regarded as the Dolphin House of the south and is located a couple of hours to the south of Hamata. This massive, horseshoe-shaped reef is home to a large population of Spinner Dolphins. Visitors to these shoals have around a 90 per cent chance of seeing them. Sha'ab Maksur is compared favourably with Elphinstone Reef and has superb walls and great drift diving amidst pristine, colourful soft corals and masses of anthias. Small schools of pufferfish are found in the evenings and you are always treated to sightings of sharks, rays and turtles.

Zabargad and Rocky Island

- Dive type: Reef wall
- Ability level: Beginner to experienced
- Depth: 5– >60 m (17– >200 ft)
- Snorkelling: yes
- Rating: ★★★★★
-

Masked Butterflyfish hang out under table corals.

Zabargad or St John's Island is the largest of the islands in Foul Bay with Rocky Island to the south her nearest neighbour. It is located 46 km (28½ miles) south-east of Ras Banas and only 40 km (25 miles) north of the Sudanese border. At over 235 m (770 ft) high, the island was once used for mining huge crystals of peridot or ancient topaz, hence the ancient Greek name for the island – Topazios. Zabargad's pinnacles are now legendary, smothered as they are in pristine soft corals and anthias. Her walls usually yield Hammerhead Sharks, Manta Rays and Silvertip Sharks. Marlin and Whale Sharks have also been seen here. Live-aboards tend to anchor in her sheltered waters and night dives are usually on the agenda as a super sand slope stretches out from the south shore and is covered in an amazing variety and size of coral pinnacles. These are little ecosystems in their own right and have a massive diversity of marine life on each one, from the larger Blue-spotted Stingrays and Crocodile Fish down to the tiniest nudibranch.

Rocky Island to the south is known for its stunning forests of soft corals and black coral trees. Huge seafans always have Long-nose Hawkfish on them as well as several species of angelfish and butterflyfish. Mantas and many species of shark are the norm here and the steep and near-vertical walls offer divers some of the best marine life vistas to be encountered in the entire Red Sea. Rarities here include the Humphead Parrotfish more commonly associated with more tropical waters and a few types of angelfish that aren't found in the north. This is superb diving.

Coral Grouper are commonly found.

St John's Reef

- Dive type: Reef, wrecks
- Ability level: Beginner to experienced
- Depth: 1– >30 m (3– >100 ft)
- Snorkelling: yes
- Rating: ★★★★★

Ghost pipefish are often seen on the reefs.

A further 20 km (12 miles) to the south-west is a series of shallow reefs, pinnacles, caverns, swimthroughs and tunnels known as St John's Reef. This is an incredibly beautiful reef system and it would take many hundreds of dives here to do it any justice, as it constantly changes with the current, the sunlight and the time of year. Sharks are here most of the year round, but when the water warms up in the summer, you get huge aggregations of emperorfish, jacks, barracudas and batfish. Abu Bassala has a huge anemone garden with hundreds of Red Sea Anemonefish.

The shallow cave system to the north is always a popular dive site as you can spend hours exploring the caves and caverns in safety. Juvenile sharks are found here as are huge moray eels, stonefish, scorpionfish, eagle rays, unicornfish and various snapper and squirrelfish. Habili Gatur, Habili Ali and Habili Gafaar have various reef platforms to explore, Dangerous Reef has just about everything that you would wish to see on every dive; Um el Gruk and many others have fantastic caverns and canyons that make for superb exploration in quite shallow water, allowing you plenty of time.

Oceanic White-tip Sharks are encountered here.

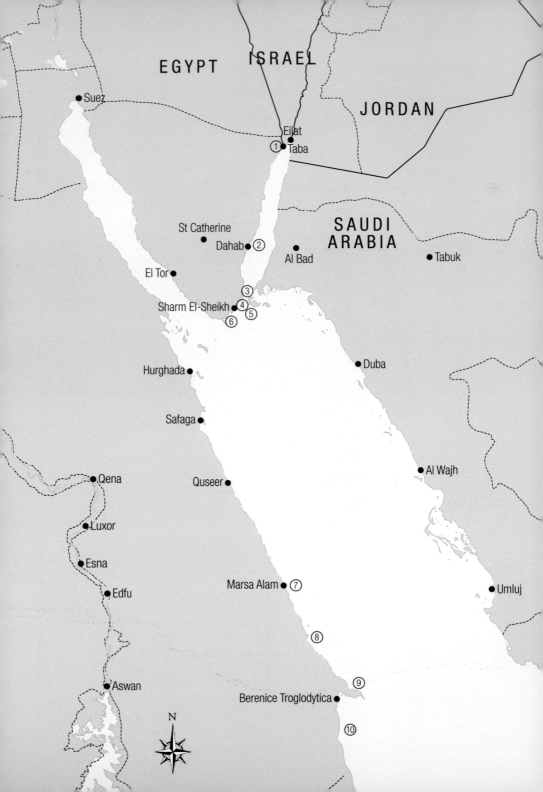

EGYPT

ISRAEL

JORDAN

• Suez

Eilat
① • Taba

SAUDI
ARABIA

St Catherine
•
• Dahab ②

• Al Bad

• Tabuk

El Tor •

③
Sharm El-Sheikh • ④
⑤
⑥

• Duba

• Hurghada

• Safaga

• Qena

• Quseer

• Al Wajh

• Luxor

• Esna

• Edfu

Marsa Alam • ⑦

• Umluj

⑧

• Aswan

⑨

Berenice Troglodytica •

⑩

N

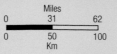

Miles
0   31   62
0   50   100
Km

Guide to Snorkel Sites

There are literally hundreds of safe snorkel sites in the Red Sea and for those prepared to do a little exploring there are even more. The sites included here are a glimpse at the best of what is available in the most popular areas.

KEY TO DIVING SITES
1. Taba
2. Dahab
3. Ras Nasrani
4. Ras Umm Sid
5. Straits of Tiran
6. Ras Muhammed
7. Marsa Alam
8. Hamada
9. Sha'ab Sataya
10. St John's Reef

Key to highlights at each site

Shark

Turtle

Macro (i.e small creatures)

Schools of fish

Ray

Coral

Soft coral

Wreck

Dolphin

Large pelagics

Dugong

Map showing location of snorkel spots.

Taba

- Type: Coral
- Ability level: Beginner to experienced
- Depth: >9 m (>30 ft)
- Rating: ★★★
- Accessibility: From the shore at all resorts
- Facilities: Hotels, dive shop, car park, toilets, restaurant

Taba has some superb shallow reefs.

Taba, the most northerly tourist destination of the 'Egyptian Riviera', has long been a favourite with divers and snorkellers. Whilst the coastline here is over-developed, there are still numerous locations where you can get away from the larger resorts. However, if you do want to swim out from the piers and jetties to the shallow fringing reef, then there are always masses of different fish species to be found in the shallows. Further to the south is the Fjord where you can swim out to the edge of the inlet and have the place virtually to yourself. Here good corals, anthias, chromis, fusiliers and Sergeant Majors predominate in the water column, but there are always interesting things out in the blue, such as turtles and rays.

The reef crest is made up of a variety of stony corals, usually *Acropora* and other reef builders. Small clams, feathery soft corals and anemones dot the reef, so there are always anemonefish to catch your attention. Parrotfish and wrasses mill around and whilst fish feeding should not be done, many of the fish here are accustomed to it and will come right up to you. Duck-diving down there are always lionfish to be found, but take care near

them and any of the Long-spined Sea Urchins. There is a hole formed here in a similar way to the Blue Hole in Dahab (see opposite), which is always of interest.

Coral or Pharaoh's Island is a short sail south from Taba and numerous tourist boats take snorkellers down for the day. You can land and explore this historic island, but with the constant dry heat, it isn't long before you start diving the fringing reef around it. The outer (eastern shore) is usually rougher on the surface, making the swim a bit more uncomfortable, but once you round the corner into the lagoon, the water is nearly always flat calm, giving you a perfect view of colourful corals, hundreds of Sergeant Majors, chromis, wrasses, parrotfish and various jacks, which sweep in from open water to attack the small schools of colourful inshore fish. Barracudas usually hang out underneath the boat, but whilst they look threatening, they are actually quite timid. You can also visit the island from the shore taking a car close to the beach from where you can swim out over a jumble of small coral heads and across the stretch of water to the island.

Dahab

- Type: Coral
- Ability level: Beginner to experienced
- Depth: >9 m (>30 ft)
- Rating: ★★★
- Accessibility: From the shore
- Facilities: Hotels, dive shop, car park, toilets, snack bar
- 🪸 🌿 🐟 ◆ 🐢

You can see why the Blue Hole is so popular.

Dahab is a popular coral reef for snorkellers. However, few venture out beyond this natural depression to the outer reef wall and lip of the Blue Hole. This is indeed incredible and has a fantastic array of soft and hard corals as well as large numbers of tropical fish. Cornetfish swim like shadows with rabbitfish, and jacks mimic the same action with one fish silver and its mate changing colour to almost black so that it acts like a shadow.

Bigfin Reef Squid are often found here, as is the Giant Puffer. Unicornfish, wrasses, parrotfish, fusiliers, Striped Butterflyfish and schools of Yellowfin Goatfish all inhabit this area. Needlefish are usually in the shallows and as you move back inside the confines of the Blue Hole area you quickly see how poor the marine life growth is, primarily due to the constant freshwater stream from the mountains that has created this natural phenomenon.

Further down the coast at Dahab's lighthouse is a huge beach area favoured by snorkellers for years as it has a very good fringing reef with large

sand chutes, where you can usually see sting rays, lizardfish, snapper and grunt as well as the usual anthias, which are so characteristic of the entire Red Sea. Many tourists and backpackers get their first taste of the wonders of the Red Sea by snorkelling here. The mountains of Jordan are in the distance as are the mountains of the Sinai behind you, making the place quite magical.

The outer reef of the Blue Hole has superb corals, best seen in the morning.

Ras Nasrani

- Type: Coral
- Ability level: Beginner to experienced
- Depth: >15 m (>50 ft)
- Rating: ★★★
- Accessibility: From the shore at all resorts
- Facilities: Hotels, dive shop, car park, toilets, restaurant
-

Acropora hard corals predominate along this stretch of coastline.

There are now around 70 piers or platforms from which you can access the outer edge of the drop-off from Nabq, south through Ras Nasrani, or Whale Bay as it was once known, and down to Na'ama Bay.

Once away from the rest of the snorkel crowd close to the resorts, you will find a steeply sloping reef swept by a gentle current, so always plan your swim with that in mind, as you may have a long swim back against the current, or have to come ashore further away than you planned.

The site is not as colourful as some, due to the predominant stony coral varieties here, but what makes these reefs special is the amount of fish to be found all the way into the shore. Schools of chromis, fusiliers, anthias, goatfish, snapper and grunt are everywhere. You will always find lionfish and scorpionfish as well as hundreds of clams and even mushroom coral. Occasionally Whale Sharks are seen here as are manta rays, but the larger coral heads will always host Coral Grouper, various butterflyfish and angelfish as well as Blue-spotted Stingrays.

Anemones and clownfish inhabit many areas of this reef.

Ras Umm Sid

- Type: Coral wall
- Ability level: Beginner to experienced
- Depth: >30 m (>100 ft)
- Rating: ★★★★★
- Accessibility: From the shore, sometimes by dive boat
- Facilities: Hotels, dive shop, car park, toilets, restaurant

To the right of the wall, small coral heads have table corals.

There are over 30 piers to the reef edge between Na'ama Bay and Ras Umm Sid, and all of them give access to the outer reef walls. Other than the heady delights of Ras Muhammed (see page 81), Ras Umm Sid is by far the best snorkel site from the shore in the south-eastern Sinai. Entry from the shore is down a well-trodden path and some steps to a wooden platform that extends to the edge of the reef where the blue water begins. It can get busy due to the nearby holiday resorts. To the left (east), the plateau gradually recedes until it joins the shoreline, to the right (west), the plateau extends much further towards the bay and the marinas at Sharm el-Sheikh.

Once you swim out into the depths, you can quickly take in the marvel of this superb coral wall that is indented with numerous caves and caverns. Schools of Glassy Sweepers can be found right up into the shallows, so there will also be lionfish and scorpionfish in the same locale. If you snorkel east, you will see a few small pinnacles and just after them are some massive seafans.

There are always small hunting parties of jacks and emperorfish here and the reef crest is where you will find different species of wrasse and parrotfish. Anthias are everywhere (as always) and you will get your first sightings of the colourful soft corals, which come in every shade, including an electric ice blue. Red and purple are the predominant colours and the whole reef just lights up as the sun passes overhead.

The access pier to the edge of the reef.

Straits of Tiran

- Type: Coral wall
- Ability level: Beginner to experienced
- Depth: >30 m (>100 ft)
- Rating: ★★★★★
- Accessibility: By day-dive or snorkel boat or live-aboard only
- Facilities: Whatever is available on board, or take your own lunch and drinks

Excellent corals and clear water are found in the Straits of Tiran.

There have been some moves to stop the snorkel day-boats from visiting the four reefs set in the Straits of Tiran due to overcrowding of the dive sites and poor conservation practices by the misuse of reef anchors, however, if you get the chance, then certainly explore both Gordon and Jackson Reefs. Thomas and Woodhouse are also great, but the former two are better.

Gordon Reef to the south has safe and easy access and the shallow sand area to the south-east is dotted with huge coral ergs made of massive stony corals and covered in Christmas

The reef as seen from up on the dive boat.

Tree Worms. Small schools of goatfish and snapper group around the sides and there are always many different species of butterflyfish and angelfish. There is also quite a large number of anemones and their anemonefish partners. If there is no current, you can even explore the wreck of the *Loullia*.

Jackson Reef to the north is simply superb. Most snorkellers hang out around the southern tip where turtles can be seen feeding on the large sponges and soft corals. Sharks often cruise the depths and it is here that you can find Lyretail Angelfish and Schooling Bannerfish, which are both quite rare in the area. The reef is very steep in some areas and also has a sand chute. Small Forster's Hawkfish are found in the shallows and there are plenty of small clams, starfish and anemones.

Ras Muhammed

- Type: Coral wall
- Ability level: Beginner to experienced
- Depth: > 100 m (> 330 ft)
- Rating: ★★★★★
- Accessibility: From the shore at all resorts or from dive boat
- Facilities: None

The reef crest starts at only 60 cm (2 ft), perfect for snorkelling.

This is probably the best snorkelling in the Red Sea. Most people snorkel here from a day boat, but Ras Muhammed is a National Nature Reserve and access is available from the shore, although there are very few or no facilities. Starting at the large headland called the Shark Observatory, the vertical wall just plummets into the depths. Best snorkelled in the morning to get the most from the sun, the reef wall is stunning and completely encrusted with colourful soft and hard corals, and masses of tropical fish. Snorkelling to the south with the wall on your righthand side, you will swim over a few large fissures that have opened up into the reef crest due to subterranean volcanic activity. Continuing on, you will eventually come to the main plateau where the three submerged reefs are found and the remains of the wreckage of the *Jolanda*.

The current can be quite strong here and there may be some surface chop, but once you are around Shark Reef, you can cut into the shallower plateau and explore the reef crest in safety. You can see free-swimming moray eels, huge Napoleon Wrasse, which, at over 2.3 m (7 ft) in length, can be quite intimidating but fantastic to swim with. The reef crest always has lots of Golden Cup Coral polyps, but the real spectacle is the main wall covered in brilliantly coloured soft corals and smothered in anthias. This is truly the iconic view of the Red Sea that everyone will remember for the rest of their lives. Just out in the blue, there are staggeringly huge schools of barracuda, bat fish, emperorfish, Black and White Snapper, unicornfish and surgeonfish. You may also glimpse sharks in the depths and this is testimony to the clarity of the water and richness of the reefs.

Colourful soft corals are also found in shallow water.

Marsa Alam

- Type: Coral bays
- Ability level: Beginner to experienced
- Depth: >9 m (>30 ft)
- Rating: ★★★★
- Accessibility: From the shore or from dive boat
- Facilities: Very few and sporadic

Dugong are found in shallow water and many snorkellers have encounters with them.

Marsa Alam/Port Ghalib is the staging post for a huge amount of coastal exploration. There are numerous marsas or bays all along the coast and, in fact, nearby Marsa Luli is rated the number one snorkel bay on TripAdvisor. Other local marsas include Marsa Agla, Marsa Abu Dabab, Marsa Morena, Marsa Mubarak, Marsa Malek and Marsa Souni Kebir. A number of the marsas have small encampments with rudimentary facilities, but most are just deserted bays with perhaps abandoned fishing huts for some shade.

The marsas are usually indented into the coastline and have protected headlands at either side, some have wide, shallow bays, some have small groups of mangroves where camels come to feed and all of them have great snorkelling. Large Green Turtles feed on the seagrass in the marsas as well as Dugong, so you may be lucky to have an encounter with these amazing creatures. The shallower lagoons and Marsa Luli, in particular, are dotted with small coral heads where anemones and anemonefish are found, along with small rays, crocodilefish and usually plenty of wrasse. I have noticed that there are large numbers of Masked Butterflyfish, which like to hang out underneath the table corals. Do keep an eye out for Titan Triggerfish, especially if they are nest building in the shallows, as they are incredibly aggressive, will chase you away from their home patch and will attack you.

Shallow sandy bays and mangroves are common in all the marsas.

Hamada

- Type: Wreck
- Ability level: Beginner to experienced
- Depth: 17 m (46 ft)
- Rating: ★★★★★
- Accessibility: From the shore, or from dive boat
- Facilities: None

Large schools of batfish are common in the southern Red Sea.

The *Hamada* is a former freighter that caught fire and sunk close to the phosphate terminal at Abu Ghoson, 68 km (42 miles) south of Marsa Alam on 28 June 1993. This wreck is rarely on the live-aboards' dive list, but as a shore dive it is a photographer's dream and is a spectacular snorkel dive as the shallowest part comes very close to the surface and the water here is only 17 m (57 ft) deep. Snorkellers get the chance to swim over an entire shipwreck that is more than 65 m (220 ft) in length. The wreck sits next to a nice fringing reef and has, in fact, become an extension of the reef as it is completely encrusted in marine life, and hosts simply thousands of fish and small invertebrates.

Lying on her starboard side, the shallowest parts of her port side are virtually at the surface. Looking down into her interior you can still see all of her cargo, which has now been claimed by marine growth. There is a lot of fire coral in the shallows, so care should always be taken around this. This wreck is on most photographers' wishlist for the southern Red Sea, but it has gained international appeal as a superb snorkel site too.

Large barracudas are seen here as are small schools of trevally, surgeonfish, Black and White Snapper, and even juvenile batfish. There appears to be more colour on this wreck probably because it is so shallow and the water so clear. It is safe for snorkelling over and a great change from some of the inshore reefs, which can often have much poorer visibility.

The shallow depth of the *Hamada* makes it perfect for snorkelling.

Sha'ab Sataya

- Type: Coral
- Ability level: Beginner to experienced
- Depth: >9 m (>30 ft)
- Rating: ★★★★★
- Accessibility: By boat only
- Facilities: Whatever is on board, but lunch and soft drinks are usually included

Spinner Dolphins are the main attraction here for snorkellers.

Sha'ab Sataya is at the top of the list for snorkellers whenever there is the chance (weather permitting) to get there. Located south of the Fury Shoals, it can take around two hours to sail there from the closest dive shop at Hamata. This horseshoe-shaped bay is also on the live-aboards' list, but it is never so busy that you will ever feel crowded. In fact, once you are in the water, you will feel that you are the only person who has ever experienced this.

Whilst the reefs have very good coral formations that are well within easy snorkelling limits, most people flock here to swim with the Spinner Dolphins. Snorkellers can also arrange to stay overnight as the lagoon is nice and sheltered, and have the same experience all over again the next day. This is what the fuss is all about!

Snorkellers cannot wait to get in the water to interact with the dolphins.

St John's Reef

- Type: Coral reef and caverns
- Ability level: Beginner to experienced
- Depth: >9 m (>30 ft)
- Rating: ★★★★★
- Accessibility: By dive boat only
- Facilities: Full service available on board

A greater diversity of corals are found in the southern Red Sea.

St John's Reef is about as far as you want to travel before you reach the Sudan. The reefs are spread out wide and have a number of farshas and habilis that come quite close to the surface, but really are too deep to spend much time on when snorkelling. However, the shallower reefs, which come virtually to the surface, are a maze of interconnecting caves, fissures and canyons that you can spend hours on, just exploring the edges of these coral structures and looking down into the depths to see the larger fish traversing the canyons. You can see whip corals, black coral trees and many different soft and hard corals. Also, being so far south, you will have a real chance of encountering the largest parrotfish on the planet, the Bumphead Parrotfish, sometimes seen in large foraging groups that tend to visit the shallows in the evenings. These huge parrotfish bite off fist-sized chunks of coral to digest the algae and animal matter within, and the resulting excretions can seriously ruin the visibility!

St John's Reef is really a collection of reefs and covers such a huge area that you will want to return time and again to explore the shallows,

as all of them are incredibly colourful, all host fantastic soft corals and countless numbers of fish. There appear to be schools of butterflyfish, angelfish, soldierfish and squirrelfish here as opposed to just the pairs that you may encounter much further north. Gorgonian seafans are also found in shallow water, so snorkellers can get the best of what most divers only see when in much deeper water. The reefs are quite exposed and the surface water may be choppy, but there are always lee shores where you can enjoy the calm clear waters of the southern Red Sea.

The deeper sections all have large seafans.

Marine Life
Identification

One of the world's most northerly coral reefs has over 1,000 different invertebrates and 200 species of hard and soft coral, which are home to 1,200 species of fish, of which 10 per cent are endemic to the Red Sea.

Parrotfish are the most colourful of all the reef fish.

Seagrass

Family Cymodocea
There are a number of different seagrasses around the shores of the Red Sea, but the most ubiquitous is the Common Seagrass (*Cymodocea rotundata*). This is the only flowering plant to be found underwater and is a vital resource as it stabilizes the seabed, provides a nursery and shelter for juvenile fish, and food for turtles and Dugong

Cymodocea rotundata

Sponges

Sponges are a very simple and ancient animal with no real tissue. They feed by drawing in nutrients from the water through tiny holes in the skin and exhaling the remains through larger holes.

Red Sea Red Sponge   *Negombata corticata*
Size: variable but usually over 30 cm (>12 in)
One of the most common sponges and where you will usually find the Pyjama Nudibranch, which feeds on it almost exclusively.

Colonial Tube Sponge   *Siphonochalina siphonella*
Size: 60 cm (>24 in)
Has a number of pale lavender or grey tubes. Often associated with coral walls and can be seen extending out from crevices. Provides shelter for fish 'sleeping' at night; fairly common on most reefs.

Phylum Cnidaria

The Phylum Cnidaria is vast and diverse, and includes soft and hard corals, jellyfish, hydroids, anemones, zoanthids and corallimorphs. Often made up of thousands of tiny individuals combining into a giant colony, there are also single, sedentary organisms, such as anemones and mushroom corals, and free-swimming species, such as jellyfish. Even jellyfish start off their lives as tiny (and attached) polyps, which look just like tiny anemones and later evolve into their free-swimming, medusa stage.

All of the species in this diverse family group are symmetrical and have a mouth/anus surrounded by tentacles armed with sting cells called nematocysts to help them snag and incapacitate their prey. Colonies such as fire corals are well named as contact with them can lead to severe irritation not unlike a bad burn.

Hydroids

Net Fire Coral *Millepora dichotoma*
Fire corals are actually hydrozoa and cousins of the true stony corals. They come in two forms. Size: variable but the tips of the branches may be only 1½ cm (½ in) This species is more finger-like and can form an irregular net, always adjacent to the prevailing current.

Plate Fire Coral   *Millepora platyphylla*
Size: colonies can be several metres across
As its name suggests, this coral consists of large, plate-like structures. Both forms are yellow/ochre in colour with white tips and both can give severe stings if you brush against them, as they fire venom from their tiny harpoons, which easily hook into bare flesh. They can form large colonies, often at the reef crest on storm-damaged reefs and shipwrecks, where there is little competition for space.

Stinging Feather Hydroid   *Macrorhynchia philippina*
Size: colonies of over 60 cm (24 in) are not uncommon
Can also cause quite a nasty sting if rubbed against. Due to their soft, attractive, feather-like formation, it is easy to forget this, hence it is always better to wear a full protective suit whilst diving.

Jellyfish

All jellyfish start life attached to a hard surface. Looking like mini anemones, they soon break free and enter into a free-swimming stage called medusa. Often at the mercy of strong currents, they are able to move themselves by pulses through their bodies. They also pack stinging cells, often found in long, trailing tentacles to capture their prey. Jellyfish provide a vital food source to marine turtles and many fish also feed on them.

Moon Jellyfish *Aurelia aurita*
Size: up to 20 cm diameter (8 in)
Blueish in colour with four distinct circles in its bell and surrounded by a ring of tiny tentacles. Most common jellyfish found in the Red Sea and not harmful to humans.

Upside-down Jellyfish *Cassiopea andromeda*
Size: 20 cm (8 in) in diameter
Has a symbiotic algae which lives in its tentacles, giving it colour. Commonly found in sheltered lagoons, near mangrove forests and shallow seagrass beds where it spends its life – upside-down – pulsing to keep it on the seabed and to drive filtered organisms into its tentacles.

The Crown Jellyfish *Cotylorhiza tuberculata*
Size: 30 cm (12 in)
Has a distinctive bell top and numerous short, stubby tentacles with a brightly coloured club tip. More often seen in the north.

Corals

Corals come in a vast and confusing number of sizes, shapes and colours. Same species are easily confused due to their divergent shapes, so I have included close-ups of a few of the less obvious species to make identification easier. Basically there are soft, leathery and hard corals, the latter including seafans and wire or whip corals. Corals are made up of two subgroups: the Octocorals and the Hexacorals, literally meaning either having eight or six tentacles per individual polyp.

Soft Corals

Vibrant Soft Coral   *Dendronephthya hemprichi*
Size: 70 cm (28 in)
Tree-like in form but grows more laterally in two dimensions and is pale pink to ochre in colour. At night, many small invertebrates can be found on it.

Klunzinger's Soft Coral   *Dendronephthya klunzingeri*
Size: 1 m (40 in)
Purple-red in colour and sometimes an icy white with blue tips. Often shrinks to half its size when not feeding. Has conspicuous calcium spicules in the skin and is home to many different invertebrates.

Leathery Corals

Common Toadstool Coral   *Sarcophyton trocheliophorum*
Size: 80 cm diameter (32 in)
Usually on a single stalk with large lobes that are smooth in nature until feeding, when the tiny, stalked, anemone-like polyps extend. Lives in well-lit reef areas.

Broccoli Coral   *Lithophytum arboreum*
Size: up to 60 cm (24 in)
Pale in colour and usually branches out from a single round stem. Often found overgrowing damaged coral. Enjoys currents and offshore reefs and at night will host several different species of invertebrate.

Pulsating Xenid   *Heteroxenia fuscescen*
Size: 16 cm (6 in)
Forms small clusters of long-stemmed, pale-coloured polyps. Most noticeable by the pumping action of their opening and closing polyps as they feed in the current.

Sea Whips & Black Coral

Black Coral Tree *Antipathes dichotoma*
Size: >3 m (>10 ft)
Creates large, tree-like formations from a single strong stem, which
may be over 20 cm (8 in). Dark greenish-brown in colour, but with a
black skeleton, it is highly prized in the jewellery trade. Home to many
other filter feeders, such as corals and winged oysters, as well as
Longnose Hawkfish.

Cluster Seawhip *Ellisella juncea*
Size: 60 cm (24 in)
Forms many large upright whips from a large communal base and
is roughly cylindrical in extent. Common on deeper reefs, but in
a well-lit position and usually in strong current, where it feeds on
passing plankton.

Spiral Wire Coral *Cirrhipathes spiralis*
Size: >2 m (>6½ft)
Common on lower reef walls, it stretches out into the current and can
be straight or spiral in formation. Unable to retract its polyps and is
home to an array of coral gobies and tiny shrimps.

Seafans

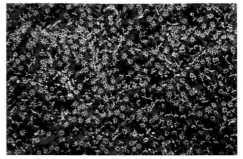

Splendid Knotted Fan Coral *Acabaria splendens*
Size: up to 1 m (40 in)
Dark red 'skin' is outlined by its white feeding polyps. Often found
in small clusters where a few individuals will grow together. Always
grows adjacent to the current.

Purple Candelabra *Pseudopterogorgia bipinnata*
Size: 60 cm (24 in)
Distinctive purple gorgonian with a good fan shape and branching
arms with purple polyps.

Fragile Yellow Net Fan *Acabaria splendens*
Size: up to 30 cm (12 in)
Pale yellow in colour with brighter yellow at each junction of the
network. Very fragile seafan, which creates a loose network of
connections and is usually found at the entrance to caverns, always
in calm water.

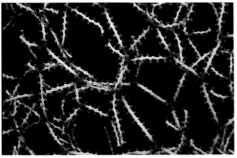

Red Crest Fragile Net Fan *Acabaria pulchra*
Size: up to 30 cm (12 in)
Identical in construction to *A. splendens* but much bushier. Has pink stems with a deeper red at each junction of the fan's network. Lives in small crevices and underhanging corals.

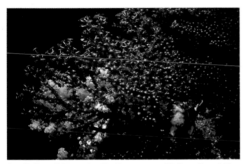

Purple Dwarf Gorgonian Seafan *Diodogorgia nodulifera*
Size: 30 cm (12 in)
Brilliant purple, small seafan, often on deeper reefs in a shaded position, or on shipwrecks. Good fan shape with wide branching arms.

Giant Seafan *Annella mollis*
Size: >2 m (>6½ ft)
Usually pale cream in colour. Often on its own on the lower reef wall below 18 m (60 ft). Widely colonized by numerous small corals and many fish use it as their home. Ras Umm Sid (see page 53) has superb examples.

Hickson's Fan Coral *Subergorgia hicksoni*
Size: <2 m (6½ ft)
Very similar to the Giant Seafan, tends to have more of its own kind around it and can form large, forest-like colonies on well-lit reef walls and always spread out into the current to catch plankton.

Hard Corals

Yellow Waver Coral *Turbinaria mesenterina*
Size: colonies can be over 2 m diameter (>6½ ft)
Very distinctive, wavy lined structure with deep valleys between each rise. Olive-green to yellow-green in colour, very knobbly in appearance as each polyp has a cone-like structure. Likes bright, well-lit water, usually in less than 18 m (60 ft) of water and known to have many different species of chromis and damselfish living on them.

Organ Pipe Coral *Tubipora musica*
Size: 30 cm (12 in)
Dark purple/red in colour, the skeleton is made up of thousands of small jointed tubes. Polyps are a pale violet or pink and easily retractable, as they are pressure sensitive. Likes well-lit, shallow reef walls and tends to extend out from the reef

Golden Cup Coral   *Tubastrea aurea*
Size: each polyp around 15 mm (½ in)
One of the most distinctive small corals to be found readily on virtually every night dive; withdraws its brilliant yellow polyps during daylight hours. Usually under coral overhangs. Can grow to many hundreds of individuals and cover large areas of the under coral.

Midnight Cup Coral Tree   *Tubastrea micrantha*
Size: up to 1 m (40 in)
Forms large branching, tree-like structures from an emerald green to a dark brown. Usually in areas of strong current, the polyps only come out to feed at night.

Bubble Coral   *Pleurogyra synplex*
Size: >1 m (>40 in)
The distinctive 'bubbles' which give this coral its name are open during the day to allow photosynthesis to take place with the blue/green algae which inhabit the coral. Skeleton is a series of sharp edges with deep fissures between. Often associated with symbiotic shrimps. At night the feeding polyps expand to catch plankton.

Acropora Table Corals

There are a number of very closely related species of this large and diverse group of corals and all of them love well-lit, shallow water to catch maximum sunshine. All grow to over 1.5 m (>5 ft) in diameter and vary just slightly in their formation. They are difficult to identify when the colonies are smaller. They create a nice shaded area beneath them and you can usually find angelfish, grouper and butterflyfish sheltering here. They are all cream or pale in colour.

Wide Acropora Table Coral   *Acropora latistella*
Stretching out like a wide coral net, quite open in structure and forms more of a fan than a circular shape.

Granular Table Coral   *Acropora granulosa*
Rougher in structure and fairly cylindrical in formation, its arms are fairly tightly packed together and covered in conical formations for the polyps.

Fuzzy Spiral Table Coral   *Acropora paniculata*
More 'fuzzy' in appearance, its tightly packed formation often creates a spiral as it stretches upwards.

Elephant Skin Coral *Pachyceris speciosa*
Size: 2 m (6½ ft)
Usually circular in shape and pale ochre in colour. Smooth underside and has concentric furrows and funnel-shaped plates. Often wedged in amongst other stony corals on the mid to deep reef, usually below 18 m (60 ft).

Secret Coral *Favites abdita*
Size: up to 1 m (40 in)
Usually brown and green in colour. Very common on all of the Red Sea reefs and will form massive interlinking colonies.

Staghorn Coral *Acropora hemprichii*
Size: colonies rarely exceed 1.8 m (6 ft) in diameter
Colonies of this shallow water coral are usually much smaller than stated above and have pale blue to pink branching arms with rounded tips. A favourite home for chromis.

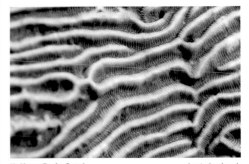

Uniform Brain Coral *Leptoria phrygia*
Size: >1.8 m (>6 ft)
Another of the massive reef builders, often a dull, pinkish-brown colour and has distinctive, elongated, raised, brain-like whorls in its formation, hence the name. The polyps only come out at night when feeding.

Cone Coral *Hydnophora exesa*
Size: up to 120 cm (47 in)
Forms massive colonies, usually in sheltered reefs, often at the entrances to some of the marsas. There are distinctive, cone-shaped formations all over the colony.

Stony coral *Pavona claevis*
Size: >3 m (>10 ft)
The third of the massive reef builders, but much more open in structure with deep fissures between the lobes of the coral structure. Often small ergs, they are usually surrounded by many other smaller coral species, but are also known to create massive aggregations giving strength and protection to a coral reef

Bristle Coral   *Galaxea fascicularis*
Size: up to 17 cm (6¾ in)
Mainly green in colour, the coral polyps are quite distinct and appear almost unattached from the rest of the colony. Fairly common throughout the region and larger colonies can grow to around 3 m (10 ft).

Scuted Mushroom Coral   *Fungia scutaria*
Size: up to 25 cm (10 in)
Always elongated or oval shaped, this single polyp coral is unattached from the reef. Has thin furrows lined with small, blunt tentacles, which funnel food to its central mouth. Prefers coral rubble slopes.

Anemones

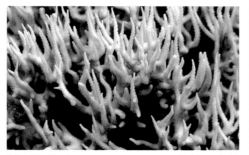

Spiny Row Coral   *Seriatopora hystrix*
Size: up to 20 cm (8 in)
Very distinctive, sharp, pointed branches, usually found in sheltered, calm water as the colony is quite fragile.

Burrowing Tube Anemone   *Cerianthus* spp.
Size: variable >12 cm (>4¾ in)
Usually transparent to pale mauve and cream in colour, body extends deep underground. Found on soft sand and fine substrate, rarely seen during the day and only extends its tentacles up through the sand when feeding at night.

Common Mushroom Coral   *Fungia fungites*
Size: up to 12.5 cm (5 in)
Distinguished by its circular shape and often found in fairly large numbers on broken corals.

Magnificent Anemone   *Heteractis magnifica*
Size: up to 1 m (40 in) in diameter
Has large, pale tentacles with a brilliant red underside. Most common anemone in the Red Sea and most commonly associated with the Red Sea Anemonefish and Three-spot Dascyllus; also known to host several species of small shrimp and even crabs. Prone to creating huge aggregations of sometimes hundreds of individuals, there are several areas of the Red Sea with well documented 'Anemone Cities'

Adhesive Anemone *Cryptodendrum adhaesivum*
Size: up to 35 cm (14 in)
Has a very sticky upper surface and is distinguished by the differently coloured outer edge. Small, shy anemone that lives amongst coral rubble or under coral boulders, where it can retreat quickly.

Carrier Anemone *Callyactis polypus*
Size: 2.5–5 cm (1–2 in)
Found only in association with the Anemone Hermit Crab (*Dardanus tinctor*) (see page 110), where the crab attaches these anemones to its shell for protection. It will transfer the anemones as it changes its shell.

Starfish

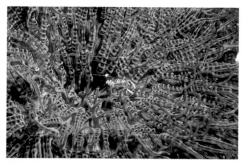

Ribbed Anemone *Heteractis aurora*
Size: 30 cm (12 in)
Many-tentacled, usually a pale olive-green in colour and has very distinctive ribs around each of its long, thin tentacles. Usually home to a variety of commensal shrimps.

Pearl Sea Star *Fromia monilis*
Size: up to 10 cm (4 in)
Has a bright red body and a chain-like pattern of cream circles, which cover each of the five arms. Note that this animal has an extra arm growing from where it was damaged.

Stinging Alicia *Alicia mirabilis*
Size: 12 cm (4¾ in)
Another anemone which shrinks down and disappears during the day, at night it extends upwards and its long, fine tentacles spread out to catch floating plankton. Knobbly protuberances on its flanks contain nematocysts tipped in venom, so stay well clear.

Tile Sea Star *Fromia nodosa*
Size: up to 10 cm (4 in)
More olive green in colour with distinctive, variable-sized, cream and brown circular markings. Often confused with the Pearl Seastar (above).

Multipore Sea Star　　　　　　　　　　*Linckia multiflora*
Size: up to 6 cm (2½ in)
This common species has five round arms and a multi-coloured orange/cream/red/white colouration, often with blue tips to the tentacles.

Sawtooth Feather Starfish *Oligometra serripinna*
Size: 22 cm (8¾ in)
Variable in colour, this crinoid comes out at night to feed and aligns its feathery arms to the prevailing current direction. Darker specimens are often found on gorgonions, where they may be out in the open all day long. It is often associated with a small, squat lobster and a specific species of crab.

Crown-of-thorns Starfish　　　　　　　*Acanthaster planci*
Size: up to 50 cm (20 in)
Known to be incredibly destructive to hard coral reefs, this very mobile large starfish eats the hard coral polyps and can lay waste if unchecked, but this is just nature's way of controlling too many hard corals. The mucous coating over the spines is poisonous.

Palm-frond Feather Star *Stephanometra* spp.
Size: up to 15 cm (6 in)
Common species, yet difficult to fully identify as it appears to have so many different colour variations. Only seen at night.

Blue Sea Star　　　　　　　　　　　*Linkia laevigata*
Size: up to 30 cm (12 in)
Large and distinctive blue starfish with long thin arms. (It also comes in a variety of other colours.) Often found in dead coral areas where it feeds on encrusting algae.

Klunzinger's Feather Starfish *Lampometra klunzingeri*
Size: up to 20 cm (8 in)
Large crinoid with over 20 multi-coloured arms and often found hanging out on the end of whip corals and seafans feeding in the current.

Savigny's Feather Starfish   *Heterometra savigny*
Size: up to 15 cm (6 in)
More uniform in colour with over 20 arms which are light and pressure
sensitive, often curling up into a tight ball if light is shined on them.

Basket Starfish   *Astroba nuda*
Size: 50 cm (20 in)
Has a central disc with five arms that repeatedly split into smaller and
smaller parts creating a huge, basket-like web, which it fully extends
when feeding. Arms are incredibly mobile, light sensitive and can curl
up very quickly. Another night feeder, spending daylight hours deep
in coral recesses.

Sea Urchins

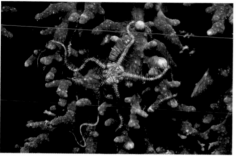

Brittle Starfish   *Ophiothrix savignyi*
Size: 15 cm (6 in)
Has five very flexible arms, used to great effect and is incredibly mobile
on the reef, generally only coming out at night to feed. Arms are very
brittle and can easily be snapped off when threatened.

Collector Urchin   *Tripneustes gratilla*
Size: 10 cm (4 in)
Colour is variable, symmetrical in shape, with clearly defined areas for
spines and tentacles. The name suggests that it often holds debris to
the top and sides of the test.

Coral Brittle Starfish   *Acanthophiotrix purpurea*
Size: up to 15 cm (6 in)
Quite mobile and has long spines along its five arms. Always found at
night on seafans, various coral species and sponges.

Toxic Leather Sea Urchin   *Asthenosoma marisrubri* (endemic)
Size: 15 cm (6 in)
Overall red in colour with long pale spines around the lower perimeter
and very mobile short spines on top separated by spineless areas.
Spines are very toxic and can cause a painful injury.

Rousseau's Coral Urchin   *Microcyphus rousseaui*
Size: 6 cm (2½ in)
Regular bands with spines and distinctive zigzag patterns in between. Quite rare locally, usually olive-green in colour as it eats Wavy Coral, which has the same colour.

Slate Pencil Urchin *Heterocentrotus mammillatus*
Size: around 30 cm (12 in) overall diameter
Main spines are thick, flattened and blunt, which it uses to wedge itself into holes in the reef. Usually a reddish-brown colour, its name comes from long ago when its spines were used as writing implements on slate boards.

Sea Cucumbers

Long-spined Sea Urchin   *Diadema paucispinum*
Size: spine length up to 30 cm (12 in)
Generally an overall black in colour with spines around 2–3 times the diameter of the body. Spines are very mobile and have a back-facing, serrated edge making them almost impossible to remove if they get stuck in your body! Anus is on top of the body and often coloured red or blue with some white spots around the outside of the shell.

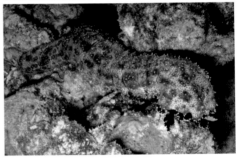

Flower Cucumber *Bohadschia graeffei*
Size: up to 1 m (40 in)
Long and mottled brown and cream, but with very obvious black, flower-like feeding 'feet' at the head. Usually on stony corals.

Rock-boring Urchin   *Echinometra mathaei*
Size: 5 cm (2 in)
Small sea urchin with numerous spines in a brown/purple colour. Lives in the reef where it bores into the old limestone. Will venture out onto the reef crest at night.

Tubercle Sea Cucumber *Thelenota ananas*
Size: up to 60 cm (24 in)
Orange-brown in colour and covered in fleshy tubercles. Always found on sand and coral rubble, often has symbiotic Imperial Shrimps about its body.

Sea Pens

Bushy Sea Pen *Penneatula* spp.
Size: up to 15 cm (6 in)
Vertically curved and oval in shape with many branching arms. Only comes up through the seabed at night to feed. Fills with water and extends its feeding tentacles to align with the current to trap microscopic plankton.

Indian Feather Duster Worm *Sabellastarte spectabilis*
Size: 10 cm (4 in)
Has branched tentacles striped with light and dark bands and lives amongst hard corals.

Tall Sea Pen *Funiculina* spp.
Size: up to 30 cm (12 in)
Very long and thin with small feeding arms, almost always pale cream or white. Similar in behaviour to *Penneatula,* these too only feed at night and both are found on fine sand or muddy bottoms.

Common Featherduster Worm *Sabellastarte sanctijosephi*
Size: up to 7.5 cm (3 in)
Very widespread with a parchment tube and spiralling horseshoe fan that opens up when feeding.

Sea Worms

Fan Worm *Sabellastarte indica*
Size: 5–10 cm (2–4 in)
Usually reddish-brown in colour, they also have pale bands. Circular whorl is all that you see of this marine worm, whose parchment tube can extend around 25 cm (10 in) under the soft sandy substrate.

Bispira Fan Worm *Bispira* spp.
Size: up to 4 cm (1½ in)
Another common fan worm that comes in a variety of colours and has a fuzzy appearance due to the multitude of very fine hairs on its arms.

Christmas Tree Worm   *Spirobranchus giganteus*
Size: 15 mm (½ in) diameter of each part
Sedentary worm, has two spiral rings of fine feathery tentacles, which
unfurl for feeding on plankton. Light- and pressure-sensitive, instantly
withdraws if you get too close, too quickly. Always found in hard
corals of some species or other and often found in large very colourful
groups. There are ten different and almost identical species in this
family, my naming is just an educated guess!

Myzostomid Worm   *Myzostomatidae* spp.
Size: up to 1.5 cm (½ in)
Very difficult to see as this semi-parasitic worm attaches itself to
the arm of a crinoid and assumes not only the colour, but the radial
lines too.

Peacock Bristle Worm   *Chloea flava*
Size: 5 cm (2 in)
Mainly on sand and gravel at the bottom of the reef, or in lagoons at
night, where it scavenges amidst the detritus. Like the Fire Worm, it
can cause a burning irritation if touched.

Red Sea Chelidonura   *Chelidonura livida* [endemic]
Size: up to 5 cm (2 in)
Long with a forked tail and a head shield with four lobes. Has brilliant
colours of iridescent blue rings and spots on a black body. Carnivorous
Aglajid that feeds on worms and small molluscs. Always found on sand
or muddy bottoms.

Tiger Flatworm   *Pseudoceros dimidiatus*
Size: up to 7 cm (2¾ in)
Very distinctly coloured. There are several species ranging from the
Red Sea to the Pacific, all with similar but slightly different markings.

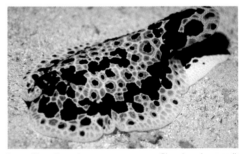

Large Pleurobranch   *Pleurobranchus grandis*
Size: up to 21 cm (8⅓ in)
Very variable in colour from a deep dark red to mottled colours of
black and grey surrounded by white rings. Member of the *Notaspidae*
(side-gill slugs) and fairly commonly seen on most night dives over
dead coral and encrusting sponges. Some family members still have a
vestigial shell within the body.

Molluscs

Nudibranchs

This a wide and diverse group, and not necessarily of the same genus, species or family, but because they all look vaguely similar, I have put together all of the various sub-species and family groups under one heading. In essence, the word 'nudibranch' means 'naked gills'. These are snails which have lost their shells and their respiratory gills (which surround the anus) are usually very obviously placed at the rear. They have a pair of sensory feelers or rhinophores at the front and a pair of eyes somewhere in the same region. They eat with the aid of rasping platelets or *radula* in a large mouth. All of the nudibranchs listed here were photographed in the Red Sea, though a few, I have since discovered, have never been officially recorded from the region.

Eyespot Wart Slug   *Phyllidia ocellata*
Size: 6 cm (2½ in)
Beautiful little wart slug, overall orange in colour with black and light blue markings between the nodules. Quite conical in shape.

Tubastrea-eating Nudibranch   *Phestilla melanobranchia*
Size: 2.5 cm (1 in)
Eats *Tubastrea* almost exclusively. It stores the polyp's stinging cells in the cerata along its back and looks exactly the same colour as the coral polyp. Common, but difficult to find.

Pustulose Wart Slug   *Phylidiella pustulosa*
Size: 6 cm (2½ in)
Overall more greyish brown in colour with paler grey nodules over all the body. Slimmer and more elongated than others of the species.

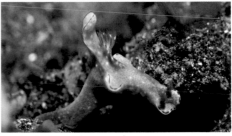

Purple-edged Ceratosoma   *Ceratosoma tenue*
Size: 11 cm (4⅓ in)
Sometimes called the Long-tailed Ceratosoma, quite a robust specimen with a wide mantle, long rhinophores and gills just at the juncture of the tail. The Red Sea population has a purple edge to its fringe.

Varicose Wart Slug   *Phyllidia varicosa*
Size: 7 cm (2¾ in)
Typically dark greyish blue with black lines between its warts that are sometimes tipped in yellow.

Twin Chromodoris   *Chromodoris geminus*
Size: 6 cm (2½ in)
With an almost luminescent colouration, the nudibranch is almost circular in shape with a darker, wavy skirt and a body covered in dark spots with a lighter lining. The gills and rhinophores are a cream to pale blue in colour.

Serpent Nudibranch   *Pteraeolidia ianthina*
Size: up to 11 cm (4⅓ in)
Very long, thin and active nudibranch. Colour is entirely dependent on its food species, as it eats algae, sea squirts and even leathery coral. Lives mainly on muddy bottoms in lagoons and near mangroves as well as amidst coral rubble.

Pyjama Nudibranch or Red Sea Slug   *Chromodoris quadricolor*
Size: up to 4.5 cm (1¾ in)
Very distinctively coloured nudibranch, usually seen on most dives where it feeds on red sponges as well as algae-covered, dead coral. Has a yellow margin with black and blue longitudinal stripes, and bright orangey yellow gills and rhinophores.

Cute Resbecia   *Risbecia pulchella*
Size: up to 11 cm (4⅓ in)
Large nudibranch, almost always crawling around in pairs, seemingly attached nose to tail. Feeds on mucus and crustose algae.

Spanish Dancer   *Hexabranchus sanguineus*
Size: up to 40 cm (16 in)
Largest and probably most familiar of the Red Sea nudibranchs. When under threat, undulates its body and swims away from trouble. With its brilliant red or orangy/red colouration and vivid white skirts, you can clearly see how it got its name. Egg cases are also very distinctive, almost like a rose flower. Has a symbiotic relationship with the Imperial Shrimp (*Periclimenes imperator*).

Octopus & Squid

Reef Octopus   *Octopus cayaneus*
Size: 1 m (40 in)
Most common octopus seen by divers and is an active feeder both during the day and at night. Lives in all marine habitats and is quite at home in the trash of a harbour, as well as in a thriving coral reef.

Hooded Cuttlefish   *Sepia prashdi*
Size: 30 cm (12 in)
Often pale in colour, able to change its body colouration and shape at will to blend in with most of its surroundings. Active hunter at night, prefers shallow lagoons, sheltered bays and coral rubble.

Reef Squid *Sepioteuthis lessoniana*
Size: up to 35 cm (14 in)
Often found in small groups where they hunt in the shallows, or just below the surface. Has the same ability as other squid and cuttlefish to change its colouration and outline skin texture. At night, they may come close to you, attracted by the food that is also attracted to your dive lights.

Shells & Snails

Squamose Giant Clam *Tridacna squamosa*
Size: up to 40 cm (16 in)
Largest bivalve in the Red Sea. Colouration of the mantle variable, but usually in hues of blue or brown. Very common on the coral reef, most are much smaller than this, as they do not have much room to expand the two halves of their shell when feeding.

Winged Oyster *Pteria aegyptiaca*
Size: 5 cm (2 in)
Distinctively shaped, this bivalve inhabits gorgonian seafans and whip corals, which both like to stretch out into the current. Attaches itself by means of Byssus threads (strong, silky fibres). Usually in small groups, they are indicative of unpolluted water.

Cock's Comb Oyster *Lopha cristagalli*
Size: up to 15 cm (6 in)
Always in small groups, it is difficult to make out each bivalve individually, as they are always covered in a growth of orange sponge or small tufts of algae and even soft corals. Has easily recognized, zigzag-shaped openings to the shell.

Red Sea Thorny Oyster Oyster *Spondylus marisrubri*
Size: 8 cm (3¼ in)
Shell is usually encrusted in algae and coral growths resembling a rough piece of dead coral. Rarely spotted during the day, feeds at night by opening its top valve slowly.

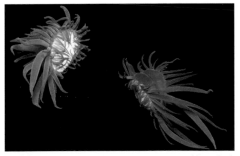

Fire Clam *Lima vulgaris*
Size: 2.5–5 cm (1–2 in)
Beautiful file clam, unattached, unlike many relatives, and will freely swim away by flapping the two identical sides of its shell to escape trouble. Looks like the body and brilliant orangey-red tentacles are too big to hide inside its shell.

Coral Scallop   *Pedum spondyloideum*
Size: up to 5 cm (2 in)
Varied in colour from pale creams to iridescent blues with red eyes.
Mostly found in folds of different species of hard corals. Holes in the
coral are kept open by a chemical secreted by the clam.

Textile Cone   *Conus textile*
Size: up to 15 cm (6 in)
Nocturnal cone shell which uses venom when hunting by spearing fish,
worms and other cone shells. Considered dangerous and its venom is
regarded as possibly fatal.

Strawberry Topshell   *Clanculus pharaoensis*
Size: 13–25 mm (½–1 in)
Has a strong, solid, slightly flattened, conical shell and is a rich dark
red with around six whorls. Each whorl has around three bands of
alternate white and dark spots. Spends most of its life around Fire
Coral.

Map Cone Shell   *Conus geographus*
Size: 6–11 cm (2½–4½ in)
Large cone shell, slightly flattened and usually with a base colour of
pale pink or cream, but with a very mottled appearance. Markings are
very intricate and the aperture is wide, allowing the striking harpoon
plenty of space when attacking fish and ingesting them whole. Highly
prized collector's shell, but its venom is known to be lethal to humans
and should be handled with extreme caution.

Red Mouth Olive   *Oliva miniacea*
Size: 5 cm (2 in)
Thick, heavy shell; bullet-shaped with a flattened spire. Body is pale,
but with many zigzag lines all over. Has a large siphon which it extends
up from a notch in the shell. Usually only seen at night.

Sand Dusted Cone Shell   *Conus tessulatus*
Size: 25-60 mm (1 – 2⅓ in)
Stout little conical shell, usually white, but tends to be overgrown
with algae, which also masks the hundreds of tiny dark dots all over
the shell that often form irregular bands. Now known to have passed
through the Red Sea and is found off the Mediterranean coast of Israel.

Reticulate Mitre   *Scabricola fissurata*
Size: 21–65 mm (¾–2½ in)
Lovely small mitre shell that can be seen at night on sand flats. Colour is variable but can range dramatically even on the one shell from pale cream with lightning flashes to a deep red at the end of the last whorl.

Umbilical Ovula   *Calpurnus verrucosus*
Size: 4.5 cm (1¾ in)
Looking remarkably like the shape of a true cowrie, has a finely spotted mantle which extends completely over the animal. Feeds on leathery corals and sponges and is often only seen at night.

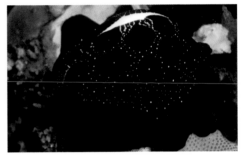

Marlinspike Auger   *Terebra maculata*
Size: 13 cm (5 in)
Regularly seen on night dives, its obvious whorls are extended out into a long spindle and coloured in bands of light brown through ochre and pale cream. Very distinctive shell that lives under the sand during the day and comes out to feed at night.

Egg Cowrie or False Cowrie   *Ovula ovum*
Size: up to 10 cm (4 in)
Another cowrie-shaped shell, usually seen in pairs. Pure white in colour but with a black mantle spotted with small white dots in circular rings. Fringe of the mantle may be blue. Found on leather corals.

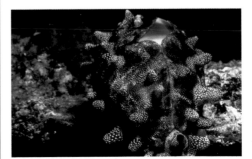

Subulate Auger   *Terebra subulata*
Size: up to 13 cm (5 in)
Covered in small dark brown spots over a creamy shell. Quite slender in form and rarely seen, except on night dives.

Talpa or Mole Cowrie   *Talparia talpa*
Size: 5–10 cm (2–4 in)
Fairly exact in their colouration of a light cream background with transverse bands of yellowish brown over the back, which blend into each other. Shell is shiny, as the mantle completely envelops the animal. Underside of the shell's 'teeth' are dark brown and the mantle is shades of grey with white dots and protruding, rounded nodules. Active at night.

Lynx Cowrie *Lincina lynx*
Size: 3.8–5 cm (1½–2 in)
Commonly found. Has a shiny shell, usually pale brown and covered in large and small dark spots. Mantle is almost transparent and has many dark spots all over, but with small, tree-like, sensory papillae that cover the entire shell.

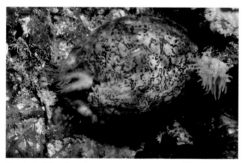

Gray's Arabica Cowrie *Mauritia grayana*
Size: 4.5–5 cm (1¾–2 in)
Like most cowries, has a smooth shiny, oval shell, usually light brown in colour with many longitudinal squiggly lines and grey spots. Has a wide aperture with dark brown teeth and mantle is almost transparent with only short sensory papillae.

Exusta Cowrie *Talparia exusta*
Size: 2.5–4.5 cm (1–1¾ in)
Smaller cowrie. Has a fairly uniform, pale cream to ochre colouration with horizontal darker ochre bands across the back. Mantle is fairly transparent with mottled brown markings and small, thin, bifurcate papillae, which are larger towards the base of this lovely rounded shell.

Crustaceans
Crabs

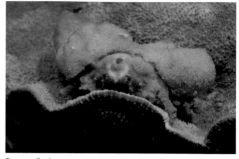

Sponge Crab *Dromidiopsis dubia*
Size: 5–7.5 cm (2–3 in)
Rather squat, pale cream-coloured spider crab with a rounded body and blunt face. Attaches the sponge to its back and holds it in place with its rear legs.

Sponge Carrier *Stilbognathus longispinous*
Size: 5 cm (2 in)
Small crab that is more spider-like in shape with thin pointed legs and claws, and a pointed rostrum. Cultivates pieces of sponge on its legs and back, and will place larger sponges onto itself for camouflage.

Splendid Coral Crab *Etisus splendidus*
Size: 7.5 cm (3 in)
Colour is quite variable from orange to red, but always a uniform colour. Active at night on the reef top, where it feeds on snails and sea urchins.

Variable Coral Crab   *Carpilius convexus*
Size: 9 cm (3½ in)
Rounded, orangeish shell, often with darker markings and purple/pink eyes. Active feeder at night, but quite shy.

Crinoid Crab   *Tiaramedon spinosum*
Size: up to 5 cm (2 in)
Only found on crinoid feather starfish, this rather spiky looking crab assumes the colour of its host and tends to stay around the base of its tentacles.

Coral Crab   *Tatralia cavimana*
Size: 2.5 cm (1 in)
Orange to cream in colour and sometimes with small spots on the shell. Lives within *Acropora* coral and is an active feeder at night, but very shy.

Soft Coral Spider Crab   *Hoplophrys oatesii*
Size: 2.5 cm (1 in)
Another highly camouflaged spider crab that lives amongst the arms of spiky soft corals. Has bits of soft coral attached to its pale pink and cream-striped shell, making it almost impossible to see.

Coral Spider Crab   *Hyastenus spp.*
Size: 3 cm (1¼ in)
Distinguished by its two long, pointed spines. Difficult to completely identify, regularly seen on night dives and is usually clear of any detritus.

Spiny Spider Crab   *Acheus spinosus*
Size: 2.5 cm (1 in)
Generally white in colour and always has pieces of sponge and algae attached to it to help in its camouflage. Most common of all the spider crabs to be found in the Red Sea. Mostly but not exclusively found on soft corals.

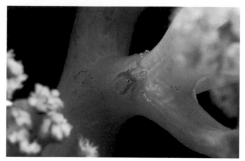

Soft Coral Squat Lobster   *Galathea balssi*
Size: 5 mm (¼ in)
Another tiny squat lobster, assuming the colour of its host soft coral and virtually transparent. Only ever seen at night.

Hermit Crabs

Anemone Hermit Crab   *Dardanus tinctor*
Size: up to 5 cm (2 in)
Size is quite variable as it depends on the size of its host shell home. Also attaches small anemones to its shell for protection and of course drags the shell and anemones around the reef looking for food scraps (which also help to feed the anemones).

Common Hermit Crab   *Dardanus pedunculatus*
Size: up to 5 cm (2 in)
Very common on the reefs and inhabits all types of abandoned shells. An active scavenger. Found in most sandy and coral rubble areas.

Rosy Hermit Crab   *Calcinus rosaceus*
Size: 2.5 cm (1 in)
An obvious little hermit crab with very dark red colouration. Usually chooses a shell which is covered in a crustose algae. Claws and legs are smooth.

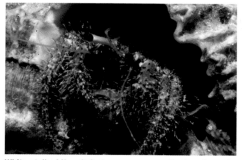

White-stalked Hermit Crab   *Dardanus lagopodes*
Size: 5 cm (2 in)
Creamy yellow to purplish brown in colour, has very spiky claws and legs, and is also covered in white hairs. Its eyes stick out on long pale stalks.

Lobsters & Shrimps

Black Coral Shrimp   *Pontonoides unciger*
Size: up to 1.5 cm (½ in)
Always taking the colour of its host whip coral, this tiny shrimp is usually in pairs and is thought to live its entire life on these whip corals.

Whip Coral Shrimp   *Dasycaris zanzibarica*
Size: up to 1.5 cm (½ in)
More robust than *Pontonoides unciger*, has two prominent 'horns' on its head and the body is deeply ribbed. Also spends its life on whip corals.

Henderson's Dancing Shrimp   *Cinetorhynchus hendersoni*
Size: up to 4 cm (1½ in)
Larger and redder in colour than *C. reticulatus*, its rostrum is hinged, rather than fixed. It too has large, very reflective eyes.

Harlequin Shrimp   *Hymenocera picta*
Size: 5 cm (2 in)
Very rare in the northern Red Sea, but more common in the south where this very distinctive shrimp lives in life-long mating pairs. Feeds exclusively on starfish.

Egyptian Prawn   *Metapenaeopsis aegyptica*
Size: 4 cm (1½ in)
Redder in colour with a short but spiky rostrum, has a steeply hinged back. Usually half-hidden in the sand, it enjoys the area at the bottom of the reef.

Green-eyed Dancing Shrimp   *Cinetorhynchus reticulatus*
Size: up to 3 cm (1¼ in)
Very obvious due to its large green eyes, which are always picked out by divers' torchlight during night dives. Its rostrum is large and spiky and points at an upward angle.

Japanese Sand Prawn   *Marsupenaeus japonicus*
Size: up to 10 cm (4 in)
Large prawn found on soft, sandy areas. Colour adapts to the substrate. The very tip of its tale has a thin blue line and its eyes are on quite long stalks to poke up above the sand when it is hidden.

Squat Cleaner Shrimp   *Thor amboinensis*
Size: 2 cm (¾ in)
Small but very distinctive cleaner shrimp with an olive-orange body
with obvious, large, iridescent spots and an upturned tail. Female is
twice the size of the male. Usually found around anemones.

Imperial Shrimp   *Periclimenes imperator*
Size: up to 3 cm (1¼ in)
Usually pinkish red or red in colour with white blotches or tiny darker
spots all over the shell and claws. Most commonly found on Spanish
Dancer nudibranchs and a number of sea cucumbers.

Painted Lady or White-banded Cleaner Shrimp *Lysmata
amboinensis*
Size: up to 6 cm (2½ in)
Very distinctive shrimp with an orangey-yellow body, red back and a
broad white stripe running down its entire length. Has highly mobile
white feelers and is an active cleaner, removing parasites from fish.

Basketstar Shrimp   *Periclimenes lanipes*
Size: 2 cm (¾ in)
Short, rounded and often with broad stripes with lighter small spots.
Also has a very pointed rostrum and is found almost exclusively on
Basket Starfish.

Common Marble Shrimp   *Saron marmoratus*
Size: up to 5 cm (2 in)
Found from the Red Sea to Hawaii, this common but shy shrimp has
a large upwards-pointing rostrum and a row of tufts of bristles down
its back and flanks. Usually a drab olive green overall but with red
splotches on the head and green-and-white spots on the flanks; legs
are banded brown and white.

Crown-of-thorns Shrimp   *Periclimenes soror*
Size: up to 2 cm (¾ in)
Very similar to *P. imperator*, but much smaller overall and has smaller
claws. More variable in colour, it is the shrimp found on the Crown-
of-thorns Starfish as well as Pincushion Starfish in the Indo-Pacific.

Banded Coral Shrimp *Stenopus hispidus*
Size: 5 cm (2 in)
Very obvious large shrimp with claws twice the size of its body and very long antennae. Claws and body are covered in tiny white hairs, and ribbed with dark red and black bands. This species is circumtropical.

Pretty Snapping Shrimp *Alpheus bellulus*
Size: 3.5 cm (1½ in)
Most colourful of the snapping shrimps found in the Red Sea with purplish-blue claws, ribbed dark bands over its back and abdomen, and sometimes two or three small yellow bands on the rear of the body.

Commensal Shrimp *Vir philippinensis*
Size: 2.5 cm (1 in)
I have only ever found this shrimp on Bubble Coral (see page 94). Transparent with tiny thin purple lines down the claws, legs and body. Has very long antennae and although quite common, is often overlooked.

Red Spot Snapping Shrimp *Alpheus rubromaculatus*
Size: 2.5 cm (1 in)
Difficult to identify until after you have taken its photograph as there are a further two very similar species found in the Red Sea. This kind has dull red markings over the entire body and claws. Digs a deep burrow in soft sand and lives in symbiosis with a few different partner gobies.

Clown Anemone Shrimp *Periclimenes brevicarpalis*
Size: up to 4 cm (1½ in)
Also referred to as the 'Peacock Tail', has a translucent body with white and purple blotches on its body, tail, legs and claws. Also has five orange spots on the tail. Found on a number of host anemones.

White-saddle Snapping Shrimp *Alpheus ochrostriatus*
Size: 2.5 cm (1 in)
Very similar to *A. rubromaculatus* but without the red markings and with two conspicuous white bands across its body and white tips to its claws.

Painted Spiny Lobster   *Panulirus versicolor*
Size: up to 40 cm (16 in)
Rather attractive spiny lobster. Juveniles identical to the adults with a pair of long white feelers, black carapace with white and yellow stripes and a greenish blue abdomen. Often only the feelers are seen extending out from a coral crevice.

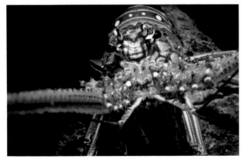

Common Spiny Lobster   *Panulirus penicillatus*
Size: 60 cm (24 in)
Fairly uniform colour of creams, reds and browns, and is particularly spiky. Largest of the spiny lobsters in the Red Sea and usually seen on night dives when it comes out of its crevice and searches the reef.

Slipper Lobster   *Scyllarides tridacnophaga*
Size: 36 cm (14 in)
Nocturnal, like most of its species. Also known as the 'Clam-Digger' due to its ability to dig up clams and shells using its plate-like frontal lobes. Like all lobsters and shrimps, it can move rapidly backwards by collapsing and flexing its tail, when danger threatens.

Copepods & Sea Spiders

Sea Spider   *Pycnogonid spp.*
Size: 1 cm (⅜ in)
Tiny creatures, usually found on fire coral. Though not a true spider, it looks just like one. Has a thin body, four eyes and walks around over the corals feeding by use of a long proboscis, which it inserts into its host to suck up the juices.

Parasitic Copepod   *Anilocra* spp.
Size: up to 1 cm (⅜ in)
Very dominant species and in some areas of the reef you will find several different species of fish with this copepod attached to the head behind the eye or near the fish's gill covers. They are more scavengers than parasites and will live their entire lives on the host fish.

Turtles

These marine reptiles spend all their lives at sea, briefly coming ashore on ancient breeding beaches to lay their eggs every few years after they reach maturity. They are all members of the *Cheloniidae*. All marine turtles are on the Red List of the IUCN (International Union of Conservation in Nature). Their nesting beaches on the Sinai have all but gone due to coastal development and much of the waste products in the sea are ingested accidentally.

Green Turtle   *Chelonia mydas*
Size: 1.5 m (5 ft)
Identifiable by having one pair of scales between the eyes and a smooth, rounded shell, one of the largest of the marine turtles found in the Red Sea and very common in the Marsa Alam area, where it shares its seagrass feeding grounds with Dugong.

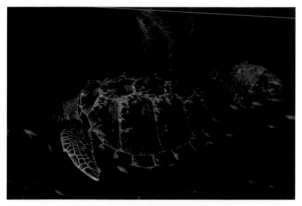

Hawksbill Turtle   *Eretmochelys imbricata*
Size: up to 1 m (40 in)
Easier to identify with two pairs of scales between the eyes and a more hooked beak. Shell plates are more defined and may have a saw-like outer edge. Feeds predominantly on sponges, jellyfish and leathery corals. Considered Critically Endangered by the IUCN. Pantropical and equally at home in the Caribbean.

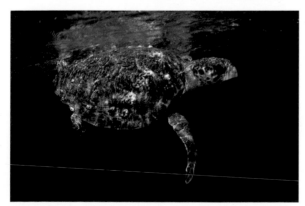

Loggerhead Turtle   *Caretta caretta*
Size: 90–270 cm (3–9 ft)
I have only ever seen this species in open water and never feeding over the reef. However, it is known to feed on jellyfish as well as bottom-dwelling invertebrates, leathery corals and sponges. Has very strong, powerful jaws and a smooth shell with five raised scutes or scales down the centre line of its back. Also pantropical.

Dolphins

These marine mammals belong to the *Cetacea* (whale) family. The dolphins found in the Red Sea are *Odontoceti* (toothed whales) and although they are not seen around reefs, they do inhabit large sheltered lagoons, of which three are well documented. These are in Sha'ab Ali; Sha'ab Samadai and Sha'ab Sataya in the far south near the Sudanese border. They are all highly sociable and will often be encountered in large groups, particularly the Spinner Dolphins down in Sha'ab Sataya. Most dolphins are pan-global; Bottlenose Dolphins are even found in British waters. Very occasionally Humpback Whales (*Megaptera novaeangliae*) stray into the Red Sea and have even been encountered off Ras Muhammed and in Dahab.

Bottlenose Dolphin   *Tursiops truncatus*
Size: 2–4 m (6½–13 ft)
Sadly this wonderful species has been very exploited and is now the main species found in captivity. Remarkably intelligent, the species is now recognised as having three distinct genus, although they are all referred to as Bottlenose Dolphins. In the Red Sea, the first glimpse of these dolphins is usually from the dive boat as it sails up the Straits of Tiran, as small pods of dolphins will ride the bow wave. Usually uniformly grey in colour with lighter flanks and belly, they have a short, well-defined snout and their 'nose' is now a blow-hole at the top of the head.

Spinner Dolphin   *Stenella longirostris*
Size 1.3–2.5 m (4¼–8¼ ft)
There at least four of five different species in the genus and all are known for their aerobatic displays. Also referred to as the Long-nosed Dolphin, the largest and most friendly pod known in the Red Sea is down in the Fury Shoals at Sha'ab Sataya. They have a slim build and triangular dorsal fin and are dark grey on the upper body almost changing to black at the tip of the snout, pectoral fins and tail. There is a distinct line between the colour change along the flanks.

False Killer Whale   *Pseudorca crassidens*
Size: up to 6 m (20 ft)
Rare but fairly frequently seen species of large-toothed dolphin. Generally black in colour and with a grey throat and neck. Known to display similar characteristics to the true Orca, by attacking and feeding on other cetaceans. Also kept in captivity. They are more commonly pantropical, but strandings have occurred in the North Sea.

Dugong

Dugong   *Dugong dugon*
Size: 3 m (10 ft)
Eating over 40 kg (88 lb) of seagrass and algae each day, Dugong, part of the *Sirenian* family, are usually easy to find by the destruction of the sandy seabed that they have just visited. It is estimated that around 4,000 live in the Red Sea and regular populations are found between Tiran Island and Sanafir, up the Gulf of Suez; Marsa Alam and further south around Suakin and the Dahlak Archipelago. They have no known predators, but are seriously under threat due to man's encroachment into their traditional feeding and nursery grounds.

Cartilagenous Fish (Rays & Sharks)

The skeletons of sharks and rays are made up of calcified cartilage and have a spinal column of 60–420 vertebrae, depending on the species. All of these fish are in the marine life group called *Elasmobranchs*. All cartilaginous fish have gills that open to the water for respiration (whereas bony fish have a bony covering to protect their gills). Some rays and sharks also breathe through spiracles, rather than gills, that are found on the top of the head behind the eyes, thus allowing them to rest on the seabed and still be able to draw in oxygenated water from above.

Blue-spotted Stingray   *Taeniura lymma*
Size: up to 1 m (40 in)
Creamy grey uniform colour with clearly defined blue spots all over the body. By far the most commonly seen ray in the Red Sea; wherever there are sandy patches on a shallow reef, you will find one, usually sheltering under a coral overhang.

Feathertail Stingray   *Pastinachus sephen*
Size: 2 m (6½ ft) including the tail
Usually a brownish cream in colour and more commonly found in shallow lagoons and near mangroves. Has distinctive, diamond-shaped pectoral fins and fleshy lobes on its tail.

Scalloped Torpedo Ray   *Torpedo panthera*
Size: up to 45 cm (18 in)
Variable in colour, but usually a uniform ochre with white and brown dotted markings. Almost circular in shape with a lobed tail. Able to stun prey with an electric charge and you will feel it if you accidentally step on one in the shallows.

Eagle Ray   *Aetobatus narinari*
Size: up to 3 m (10 ft) including the tail
Uniform greyish black in colour with irregular white circles and spots all over its upper body. Likely to be solo, swimming past the outer reef edge, but more commonly to be found in the lagoons where they hunt molluscs and crustaceans by shovelling into the sand with their pointed snouts.

Manta Ray   *Manta birostris*
Size: up to 5 m (17 ft)
By far the largest ray to be found in the Red Sea and whilst very
rare, it can often be seen cruising the outer edges of any prominent
coral points and islands. Almost always black on its upper body and
white underneath, the belly often has identifying markings. Has huge
triangular 'wings' and large, lobed appendages out front, which it can
unfurl to help direct plankton into its massive mouth.

Tiger Shark   *Galeocerdo cuvier*
Size: 5 m (17 ft)
I had my first encounter with a Tiger Shark at the southern tip of Shag
Rock in 1983 and that memory still stays with me. A fairly uniform grey
in colour with a white belly and dark stripes down its body that fade
with age. This *Requiem* shark has a blunt nose and forward-facing
eyes that allow it much more special vision. Usually a solitary hunter,
although small groups will come together if there is enough food in
the water. Eats anything!

Whitetip Reef Shark   *Triaenodon obesus*
Size: 2 m (6½ ft)
Has elongated body with white tips to its dorsal fin and a uniform grey
body on top gradually getting lighter towards the underside, usually
with a number of dark spots on its flanks. Often observed lying on the
seabed or in small caves and I have personally found Whitetip caves
up on Shag Rock and on Jackson Reef.

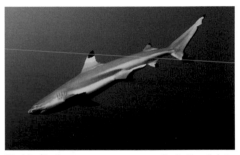

Blacktip Shark   *Carcharhinus limbatus*
Size: 1.8 m (6 ft)
Brownish grey in colour, has a white belly and distinctive black tips
to all of its fins and tail. Relatively small shark more common in the
southern Red Sea where it enjoys roaming along the edge of the deep
reefs and vertical walls.

Tawny Nurse Shark   *Nebrius ferrugineus*
Size: 3 m (10 ft)
Large stout shark with a rounded, blunt nose and fleshy barbels under
its mouth. Usually dark grey or brownish green in colour. A bottom
feeder of carrion as well as small fish, crustaceans and squid, which
it hunts at night. During the day can be found under coral ledges.

Oceanic Whitetip Shark   *Carcharhinus longimanus*
Size: up to 3.5 m (11½ ft)
Quite heavy looking with a large, rounded dorsal fin and large tail with
distinctive white markings on the tips of all of its fins and tail. Also
has a sharply defined snout. At home in the southern Red Sea and
regularly seen off the Brothers Islands; Elphinstone and Daedalus.

Silvertip Shark *Carcharhinus albimarginatus*
Size: 3 m (10 ft)
More slender than Oceanic Whitetip and whilst it also has a white tip to its tail and dorsal fin, its dorsal fin is much more triangular. Its snout is more rounded. Much rarer to find as it is quite shy, but we have found them off the Brothers Islands and deep down off Elphinstone.

Thresher Shark *Alopias vulpinus*
Size: up to 6 m (20 ft)
Dark blue/grey above and has a white underside. Has a very obvious, elongated upper lobe to its tail and large dorsal fins. I have only ever found this shark at one site and that is off the deep plateau of the southern tip of Little Brother Island.

Silky Shark *Carcharhinus falciformis*
Size: 3 m (10 ft)
Sleek in appearance with a pointed snout, a triangular dorsal fin and long pectoral fins. Pelagic shark, usually encountered off the offshore reefs and small islands. Often found in small hunting packs, they are quite curious and may come close.

Whale Shark *Rhincodon typus*
Size: up to 12 m (40 ft)
One of the most obvious sharks of all with its huge, blunt head and ribbed body covered in white and grey spots. I have seen one on my last three trips to the Red Sea: off Tiran Island, Ras Nasrani and Ras Zatar. The largest fish in our seas and circumtropical, feeding on plankton and tiny fish which it follows during the large tidal movements of plankton. Almost always accompanied by pilotfish, cobias and numerous remoras.

Bony Fish

Over 90% of all other fish in our seas, rivers and lakes are bony fish. Basically what sets them apart from cartilaginous fish is their bony skeleton and the large bony plate that protects the gills. Most fish also have distinct rays or spines on their fins. Ray-finned fishes are referred to as *Actinopterygii* and lobe-finned fishes as *Sarcopterygii.*

Angelfish

Regal Angelfish *Pygoplites diacanthus*
Size: 25 cm (10 in)
Oval-shaped fish unmistakeably coloured with vertical bands of luminescent blue and black on a brilliant yellowish orange background. One of the most colourful fish in the Red Sea.

Lyretail Angelfish *Genicanthus caudovittatus*
Size: 20 cm (8 in)
Males and females have different colouration: the male has vertical black stripes over a pale grey body and a long dorsal fish and the female a more pinkish hue to the body, a dark smudge above the eye and two stripes which accentuate the lyre tail. They have a white dorsal fin and I have found them below 30 m (100 ft) at the southern point of Jackson Reef.

Emperor Angelfish *Pomacanthus imperator*
Size: up to 40 cm (16 in)
Synonymous with the Red Sea, usually in their life-long mating pairs and prefer areas with seafans and many coral ledges and crevices where they can hide easily. Quite territorial. Juveniles always on their own and have a totally different colouration of a deep blue background with concentric white swirls around the flanks of the body.

Barracuda

Arabian or Blue Angelfish *Pomacanthus maculosus*
Size: up to 50 cm (20 in)
Large and solitary angelfish with an overall blue body becoming pale yellow at the tail. Has a very distinctive, large, bright yellowish orange splash of colour on both flanks midway along the body.

Blackfin Barracuda *Sphyraena qenie*
Size: 130 cm (51 in)
Long and sleek, its chevron markings are very prominent. Commonly seen in large shoals around coral headlands, such as Ras Muhammed. Most prolific in the Red Sea and hangs out in the current waiting for sunset before hunting.

Great Barracuda *Sphyraena barracuda*
Size: >1.8 m (>6 ft)
Always on its own and enjoys scaring the life out of divers as it comes quite close whilst you are exploring shipwrecks. Looks very dangerous but is not – to us!

Batfish

Circular Batfish *Platax orbicularis*
Size: up to 50 cm (20 in)
Circular in shape with rounded fins getting larger towards the tail. Has vertical dark bands along front of its flanks and lacks the distinctive dark spot found on the very similar Longfin Batfish (below).

Longfin Batfish *Platax teira*
Size: up to 50 cm (20 in)
Named after the long fins in juveniles; adult form is distinguished from *P. orbicularis* by the dark irregular spot/blotch just behind and below the pectoral fin. Often in small groups.

Blennies

Scale-eating Sabretooth Blenny *Plagiotremus tapeinosoma*
Size: 14 cm (5½ in)
Long and slender, with dark stripes and a full length dorsal fin. Voracious; generally hovers near the bottom and around known cleaning stations where it will make a sneak attack on any unwary fish and take a bite out before quickly retreating.

Black-lined Fang Blenny *Meicanthus nigrolineatus*
Size: 9 cm (3½ in)
Another of the voracious little flesh-eating blennies. Pretends to be the much more benign Red Sea Mimic Blenny (below) allowing it to get close to prey, before taking a chunk out of them.

Red Sea Mimic Blenny *Escenius gravieri*
Size: up to 8 cm (3¼ in)
Has a blue head blending into a pale yellow rear with a dark line just under the dorsal fin. Has the opposite defence mechanism from the Black-lined Fang Blenny, in that it pretends to be the aggressive flesh-eater and even swims the same way, hence keeping would-be predators at bay, just in case it gets bitten.

Blue-striped Sabre-toothed Blenny *Plagiotremus rhinorhynchus*
Size: 12 cm (4¾ in)
Greenish yellow in colour with iridescent blue, longitudinal stripes along the body. A mimic of the Cleaner Wrasse (*Labroides dimidiatus*) and hides in old worm tubes in the hard coral. Once a suitable prey comes close, it pretends to be a cleaner wrasse, but takes a chunk out of the fish instead and quickly retreats to its hole.

Chestnut Blenny *Cirripectes castaneus*
Size: up to 12.5 cm (5 in)
Overall chestnut brown in colour with reddish markings and stripes. Large but shy blenny, usually well hidden in coral crevices. Has distinctive small 'antlers' just behind the eyes at the top of its head.

Red Sea Combtooth Blenny *Escenius dentex*
Size: up to 6.5 cm (2½ in)
One of the most common blennies and very obvious on the outside of corals as it is so busy. Has starry eyes, golden-dotted forehead and gold and brown longitudinal stripes along its body.

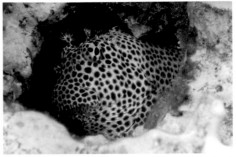

Leopard Blenny *Exallias brevis*
Size: 14 cm (5½ in)
Easily identified by the leopard spots all over the body. Spots change from black to reddish brown towards its wide tail. Has a large head with small branching 'antlers'.

Butterflyfish

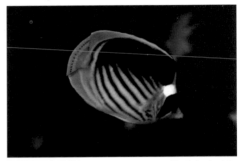

Striped Butterflyfish *Chaetodon fasciatus*
Size: 23 cm (9 in)
This distinctive fish is oval in shape, yellow with dark diagonal stripes running to the long dorsal fin. Has a black mask over its eyes, with a white patch above. Seen in pairs and small groups of 12–20 fish in the afternoons at the reef crest.

Polyp Butterflyfish *Chaetodon austriacus* [endemic]
Size: 13 cm (5 in)
Oval in shape with yellow lower flanks leading to white upper; dark tail and vertical stripes through the eye. Loves coral-rich areas in shallow lagoons and feeds on coral polyps. Always in a mating pair and usually associates with other butterflyfish.

Red Sea Bannerfish   *Heniochus intermedius*
Size: 20 cm (8 in)
Has a very obvious snout and raised eyebrows with a black face on a yellow body and dark diagonal band running from under the tail to the start of its white dorsal fin. Active species, usually seen in pairs and tends to hang out under table corals during the day amongst other butterflyfish and angelfish.

Masked Butterflyfish   *Chaetodon semilarvatus*
Size: 23 cm (9 in)
The most conspicuous of the Red Sea butterflyfish with its bright yellow body, pale orange vertical bars and blue/grey splotch of colour behind the eyes.

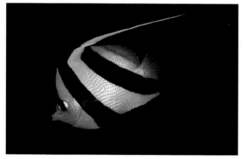

Schooling Bannerfish   *Heniochus diphreutes*
Size: 18 cm (7 in)
Similar to the Red Sea Bannerfish, has a white body, long snout, no 'eyebrows' and long thick dorsal fin. Also has black diagonal stripes, but has a pale yellow tail. Usually found below 30 m (100 ft).

Black-backed Butterflyfish   *Chaetodon melannotus*
Size: 15 cm (6 in)
Has a black ocular band that hides the eye, dark diagonal strips on a white body and yellow fins and tail. Feeds on coral polyps. Shy, rarely seen on the outer reefs and prefers more sheltered shallow lagoons.

Lined Butterflyfish   *Chaetodon lineolatus*
Size: 30 cm (12 in)
Largest of the genus and loves lagoons and seaward-facing reefs. Has a white body with thin, dark vertical bands, and a black and yellow dorsal fin and yellow tail. Always in pairs and feeds on coral polyps and small anemones.

Yellow Longnose Butterflyfish   *Forcipiger flavissimus*
Size: 22 cm (8¾ in)
Easily identified by its elongated snout used to pick at small coral polyps. Snout is black on top and white below, with the bulk of the rest of the body a uniform yellow. Also has a small black spot just before the tail.

Chevron Butterflyfish   *Chaetodon trifascialis*
Size: up to 18 cm (7 in)
Small territorial fish with a white body, chevron dark stripes, black tail, ochre fins and a black ocular band outlined in white.

Threadfin Butterflyfish   *Chaetodon auriga*
Size: 18 cm (7 in)
Has white body, dark chevron stripes and yellow hind quarters, tail and long dorsal fin. Subspecies *C. auriger setifer* has a dark spot just before the tail.

Red-backed Butterflyfish   *Chaetodon paucifasciatus*
Size: 14 cm (5½ in)
Has an elongated snout, chevron markings on its flanks and distinctive dark red/brick patch of colour just before the tail and at the tip of its broad tail. Always in pairs or loose groups and associated with other fish of the same genus. Enjoys small coral heads near seagrass beds and will cover large areas in search of food.

Cardinalfish

Iridescent Cardinalfish   *Apogon fraenatus*
Size: 12 cm (4¾ in)
Silvery transparent with a pale blue blush and one long dark stripe down the body. Widespread, always solitary and likes small coral heads in sandy lagoons. Leaves the reef when feeding at night.

Orangehead Butterflyfish   *Chaetodon larvatus*
Size: up to 12 cm (4¾ in)
Has an orange face, chevron stripes along a pale grey body and black at the rear of the fins and tail. Mainly in mating pairs amongst good *Acropora* coral growth where it feeds on polyps.

Spinyhead Cardinalfish   *Apogon urostigma*
Size: 15 cm (6 in)
Usually has an obvious dark line edged in iridescent silvery blue along the body. First dorsal fin has a black front edge and second is translucent and larger.

Orange-lined Cardinalfish   *Archamia fucata*
Size: 10 cm (4 in)
Usually an olive green in colour with lighter vertical bands and iridescent lines from snout to eye. Enjoys sheltered bays and lagoons and often seen in large numbers, all hanging out together amongst branching corals.

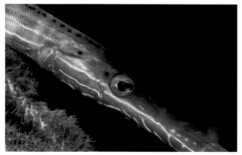

Fiveline Cardinalfish   *Cheilodipterus quinquelineatus*
Size: up to 12 cm (4¾ in)
As the name suggests, it has five distinct horizontal stripes on each side of its body. Often in small to large groups amongst open coral reef ledges with lots of crevices to hide in. Unlike some of the others in this family, this fish is also active during the day.

Coronetfish & Needlefish

Coronetfish   *Fistularia commersonii*
Size: 150 cm (5 ft)
Changes colour regularly from brilliant yellow, through silver to dark orangey red. Usually on its own, but often accompanies other fish, such as trevally or rabbitfish, where it acts as a shadow, picking up food scraps on the way.

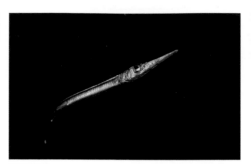

Needlefish   *Tylosorus choram*
Size: up to 130 cm (4¼ ft)
Has a long, thin and silvery body with a long snout. Pelagic species and enjoys coastal waters, particularly over the reef crest where it feeds on juvenile fish.

Damselfish, Anemonefish & Chromis

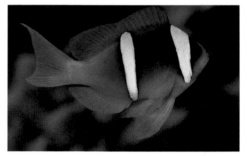

Red Sea Anemonefish   *Amphiprion bicinctus* [endemic]
Size: up to 11 cm (4⅓ in)
Mainly uniform orangey yellow in colour with two broad, iridescent vertical stripes down the fore body. Often referred to as the Red Sea Clownfish, the larger the anemone host(s), the larger the fish and the greater numbers of fish to be found. Happy to share their anemone homes with *Dascyllus*, small cleaner shrimps and anemone crabs. Territorial, will come out and attack you if you get too close.

Arabian Dascyllus   *Dascyllus marginatus*
Size: up to 6 cm (2½ in)
Has a pale blue body, black dorsal and anal fins, and yellow face. Occurring singly, in pairs or only very small groups. Lives in branching corals in shallow lagoons.

Humbug Dascyllus   *Dascyllus aruanatus*
Size: 8 cm (3¼ in)
Rarer than other *Dascyllus* in the Red Sea. White with three very distinctive, broad, vertical black bars on its body connecting its caudal fin to its ventral fins. Usually in shallow water on the reef crest; amidst branching corals.

Bicolor Puller   *Chromis dimidiata*
Size: 8 cm (3¼ in)
Very distinctive. Has a dark head and fore body, leading to a white rear and tail. Usually on its own or in small groups just above the coral.

Three-spot Dascyllus   *Dascyllus trimaculatus*
Size: 12 cm (4¾ in)
Dark grey to black in colour and loses its spots as it reaches maturity. Closely associated with the Red Sea Anemonefish and will live in the same host anemone with them.

Jewel Damselfish   *Plectroglyphidodon lacrymatus*
Size: up to 15 cm (6 in)
Uniform dark green in colour with brilliant blue spots on the face (and the rest of the body in juveniles). Large and territorial. Found amongst algae, mangrove forests and seagrass beds.

Blue-green Puller or Green Chromis   *Chromis viridis*
Size: 10 cm (4 in)
Green towards aquamarine in colour and very common amongst branching corals, which it darts into as danger approaches. Feeds on passing plankton and shelters in the coral head at night.

Lemon Damsel   *Pomacentrus sulfureus*
Size: up to 11 cm (4⅓ in)
Uniform yellow over its body and fins with just a black spot at the base of its pectoral fin. Very common on most shallow reefs.

Pale Damselfish   *Amblyglyphodon indicus*
Size: 8 cm (3¼ in)
Similar to *A. flavilatus*, but without the pale yellow colouration. Usually has its spiky dorsal fins up and is very territorial on the reef.

Indo-Pacific Sergeant Major   *Abudefduf vaigensis*
Size: up to 17 cm (6¾ in)
Very similar to *A. sexfasciatus* but with yellow colouration between the black bands across the flanks. Very common on all of the reefs and usually seen in large schools near the surface, feeding on plankton or tidbits from snorkellers.

Eels

Yellowside Damselfish   *Amblyglyphodon flavilatus*
Size: 8 cm (3¼ in)
Similar to *A. indicus* above, but with a very distinct pale yellow colouration in juveniles, changing to paler yellow on the rear of the flanks in adults. Also very territorial.

Striped Eel Catfish   (*Plotosus lineatus*)
Size: 30 cm (12 in)
Typical catfish structure with eight distinctive barbels around the mouth. Usually dark brown to almost black in colour with two broad white stripes running each side from its snout to the tail. Juvenile and young adults are always found in tightly packed groups when feeding along the seabed. It has three venomous spines and sensory ampullary canals, similar to those found on sharks.

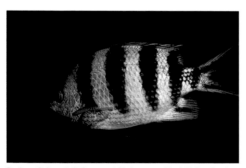

Dark or Scissortail Sergeant Major *Abudefduf sexfasciatus*
Size: up to 14 cm (5½ in)
Slightly smaller than *A. vaigensis* and more silvery grey in colour with darker black vertical bands and no yellow on the flanks. Has obvious dark lines at top and bottom of tail fin.

Garden Eel   *Gorgasia sillneri* [endemic]
Size: up to 42 cm (16 ½ in)
Always found on shallow sandy slopes and near seagrass beds. Can have huge colonies of over 1,000 gently waving in the current with their tails still tucked into the burrows and their heads and bodies swaying to catch planktonic tidbits. Retreats into its burrow whenever you get too close.

Moustached Conger Eel   *Conger cinereus*
Size: up to 80 cm (32 in)
Grey with dark brownish bands along the body. Shy; appears to enjoy a habitat at the bottom of the reef or in shallow lagoons with small coral heads, where it hunts for small sleeping fish at night.

White-eyed Moray Eel   *Siderea thysoidea*
Size: 65 cm (26 in)
Light tan to brown in colour with brownish mottling and large silvery white eyes. Shy; often taking up residence in the holes of other eels.

Snowflake Moray   *Echidna nebulosa*
Size: up to 80 cm (32 in)
Has distinctive dark blotchy bands with yellow spots, a white nose and yellow nostrils. Fairly widespread and usually found in shallow water where it is an active feeder at night.

Yellowmouth Moray   *Gymnothorax nudivomer*
Size: 180 cm (6 ft)
Large eel; pale greyish tan colour, covered in darker spots. Inside of mouth is a bright yellow.

Peppered Moray   *Siderea grisea*
Size: 65 cm (26 in)
Distinctive light grey body with a pale blue long fin and geometric dark spots around the head and between the eyes. Often found in small groups, sharing a den with other species of moray.

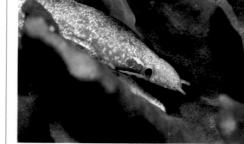

Undulated Moray Eel   *Gymnothorax undulatus*
Size: 150 cm (5ft)
Long and active eel with prominent nostrils. Enjoys shallow lagoons, wrecks and reef edges, where it hunts at most times of the day.

Giant Moray *Gymnothorax javanicus*
Size: up to 3 m (10 ft)
Largest eel to be found in the Red Sea. Brown to dark grey and mottled with darker spots. Usually out in the open and even free-swimming over the reef. Feeds on sleeping fish and crustaceans. Its poor eyesight allows divers to get quite close.

Flounders

Leopard Flounder *Bothus pantherinus*
Size: up to 35 cm (14 in)
Male has long filaments that lead to the caudal fin. Greyish in colour with irregular dotted markings over its upper surface. Usually on fine sandy seabeds and slopes amongst small coral heads, but not on the coral.

Blackspotted Sole *Aseraggodes melanostictus*
Size: 18 cm (7 in)
Fairly uniform brown in colour with brownish to black spots over its upper body. Rarely seen in the Red Sea, except in the south.

Frogfish, Seahorses, Pipefish, Clingfish & Shrimpfish

Striped Clingfish *Diademichthys lineatus*
Size: 6 cm (2½ in)
Long and thin body, purplish brown in colour with broad pale horizontal stripes. Very similar in behaviour to the Arrow Blenny in the Caribbean. Lives amongst seagrasses and sea urchin spines and can quickly move by a flick of its tail.

Coral Shrimpfish *Aeoliscus strigatus*
Size: 5 cm (2 in)
Colourful, but with a metallic silvery sheen. Forms small hunting groups, swimming head down around the reef.

Ornate Ghost Pipefish *Solenostomus paradoxus*
Size: up to 12 cm (4¾ in)
I was first introduced to this most exotic fish back in 1983 in the Near Garden at Na'ama Bay (see page 51) and have loved the species ever since. A member of the pipefish and seahorse family, female incubates the eggs. Superbly camouflaged amongst soft corals and virtually disappears when among them.

Robust Ghost Pipefish *Solenostomus cyanopterus*
Size: 15 cm (6 in)
Variable in colour, but always in muted tones of brown to ochre. Has a long snout, narrow body, and broad fins and tail. Often found in seagrass.

Slender Pipefish *Trachyrhamphus longirostris*
Size: up to 40 cm (16 in)
Usually a grey/brown in colour and often covered in a patina of fine algae. Likes muddy bottoms and mangrove lagoons.

Network Pipefish *Corythoichthys flavofasciatus*
Size: up to 14 cm (5½ in)
Has a short, pinkish snout and dark bands down the length of its body, turning to a deep purple. Usually found in pairs on coral rubble.

Black-breasted Pipefish *Corythoichthys nigripectus*
Size: up to 11 cm (4⅓ in)
Orangey red in colour with delicate red stripes and yellow spots along its banded body. Has a fan-like tail. Always in pairs in small coral caves and crevices.

Schultz's Pipefish *Corythoichthys schultzi*
Size: up to 16 cm (6¼ in)
Has a very long snout. Much paler in colour than other pipefish found in the Red Sea. Widespread. Always in pairs or even small groups when it comes into roost amongst seafans.

Ringed Pipefish *Dunkerocampus boylei*
Size: up to 17 cm (6½ in)
Fairly rare. Has wide vertical bands of reddish black with silvery white between. Has a red fan-shaped tail. More often seen late afternoon or evening.

Spotted Seahorse *Hippocampus fuscus*
Size: up to 30 cm (12 in)
Colouration depends on the habitat and food diet. Always found on algae and seagrass beds, not found on coral.

Painted Frogfish *Antennarius pictus*
Size: up to 21 cm (8⅓ in)
Highly variable colour variations, making it not only difficult to identify, but also very difficult to find. With their hanging lure, it is difficult for any small prey to resist.

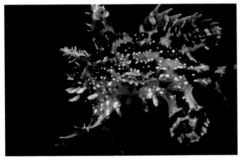

Sargassum Frogfish *Histrio histrio*
Size: up to 20 cm (8 in)
With superb cryptic camouflage and resembling Sargassum weed, this weirdly shaped frogfish is a rare visitor to the Red Sea, but is becoming more frequent. A superb predator using its lure to attract its prey, including other frogfish.

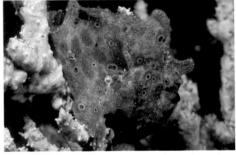

Freckled Frogfish *Antennarius coccineus*
Size: up to 12 cm (4¾ in)
Distinguished by the darker spots along its flanks. Has loose, prickly skin often covered with filamentous extrusions, adding to its camouflage as algae gets stuck to these parts. Always sitting still amongst corals or sponges.

Shaggy Anglerfish *Antennarius hispidus*
Size: up to 20 cm (8 in)
Very fuzzy in appearance and covered in tiny filamentous hairs to which algae attaches. Colour is very variable and will have hues of purple, pink, brown, ochre and everything else in between. Enjoys fairly shallow water near habours and marinas.

Giant Frogfish *Antennarius commersoni*
Size: up to 38 cm (15 in)
Generally a pale yellow or orangey yellow in colour. By far the largest frogfish, it has been found as far north as Taba, near the Israeli border, yet is also found as far south as the Fury Shoals. Can be found in most habitats, but appears to enjoy water less than 18 m (60 ft) deep.

Goatfish, Mullet & Remora

Red Sea Goatfish   *Parapeneus forsskali*
Size: up to 28 cm (11 in)
Has a distinctive grey upper body, separated from the white lower body by a dark band and an obvious dark spot, just in front of its yellow tail. Generally the most common of the shallow water goatfish found in the Red Sea, usually around the base of the coral reef.

Fringe-lip Mullet   *Crenimugil crenibalis*
Size: up to 60 cm (24 in)
Silvery coloured with large scales and horizontal dark silver stripes. Usually in large schools of a hundred or more. Found in shallow coastal waters and feeds on detritus that collects on old coral or rocks.

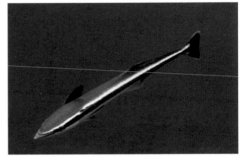

Yellowsaddle Goatfish   *Parupeneus cyclostomus*
Size: up to 50 cm (20 in)
Large goatfish. Often coloured greyish pink. Associates with similar species. Usually swimming in large shoals above the coral reef and coral rubble areas.

Striped Remora   *Echineus naucrates*
Size: up to 80 cm (32 in)
Overall grey in colour with horizontal dark and pale stripes and an obvious sucker disc on top of the head. Most abundant sharksucker; can be found with any and all large animals, fish and mammals including Manta Rays; Dugong, turtles and Whale Sharks.

Gobies

Yellowfin Goatfish   *Mulloides vanicolensis*
Size: up to 38 cm (15 in)
Has a yellow stripe running back from eye to yellow tail. Very common throughout the area and often in massive schools.

Gorgonian Goby   *Bryanopsis tigris*
Size: 4 cm (1½ in)
Has darkish red/brown bars and numerous spots on its flanks. Always found on whip corals where an adult pair will live their entire lives, even eating away some of the coral polyps to lay their eggs. Once hatched, the coral regrows over the stem.

Whip Coral Goby *Bryanopsis yongei*
Size: 3 cm (1¼ in)
Very similar to *B. tigris*, also lives on whip corals, but is smaller and has a more pronounced snout. Also more translucent and has no obvious spots.

Citron Goby *Gobiodon citrinus*
Size: up to 7 cm (2¾ in)
Large, lemon yellow with quite a big head and two to four vertical, electric blue stripes down its head. Resembles an anemonefish. Often only found on its own, off Marsa Alam there are some coral areas where a dozen or more all stay together and perch.

Michel's Host Goby *Pleurosicya micheli*
Size: 3 cm (1¼ in)
Almost translucent, with an obvious line running down its body. Tends to live on the stalks of soft corals and small sponges.

Orange-dashed Goby *Valenciennea puellaris*
Size: up to 14 cm (5½ in)
Quite robust with large orange spots and around six orangey vertical bars. Always on sand or coral rubble, usually found in pairs.

Tailspot Goby *Amblygobius albimaculatus*
Size: up to 13 cm (5 in)
Has two dorsal fins; the first tall and spiky, the second more rounded with three obvious spots. Rest of the colouration is mixed blues and greyish browns. Lives in the sand rubble and is always associated with a partner shrimp.

Steinitz's Shrimpgoby *Amblyeleotris steinitzi*
Size: 8 cm (3¼ in)
Pale with dark eyes on an ochre-striped body. Found in association with a number of partner snapping shrimp, where they share the same burrow.

Grouper, Basslets & Dottybacks

Merten's Shrimpgoby   *Vanderhorstia mertensi*
Size: up to 10 cm (4 in)
Has finely speckled gold spots on its fore body and several dark chestnut bands down its body. Usually in very silty, sandy areas. Always with an *alpheid* shrimp.

Marbled Grouper   *Epinephelus polyphekadion*
Size: up to 65 cm (26 in)
Overall pale grey in colour with darker grey spots and blotches all over the body and head. Usually found amongst protected inshore reefs, tends to hide amongst the coral and along the base of the reefs.

Blackfin Dart Goby   *Ptereleotris evides*
Size: up to 14 cm (5½ in)
Usually seen in small groups or pairs and though they are a benthic fish, they spend their time well off the bottom where they feed on plankton.

Blacktip Grouper   *Epinephelus fasciatus*
Size: up to 40 cm (16 in)
Has a light body, orangey brown lateral stripes, a darker area above the head and distinct black tips to its dorsal fin. Common in all areas, but particularly on reef flats, coral rubble and sand slopes.

Red Fire Goby   *Nemateleotris magnifica*
Size 6 cm (2 ½ in)
Once considered rare, a distinctive, burrowing goby with a white head changing to deep red at the tail, and a long dorsal fin. Almost always seen in pairs.

Greasy Grouper   *Epinephelus tauvina*
Size: up to 70 cm (28 in)
Has brownish pink spots on a pale grey to dull white body. Spots become more concentrated towards the head. Quite common, it is always busy on the reef, and can be approached quite easily.

Red Sea Coral Grouper   *Plectropomus pessuliferus marisrubri*
Size: up to 1.1 m (43½ in)
Purplish pink in colour with darker blue spots, which may form a few vertical bands down its flanks. One of the largest of the Red Sea grouper. Very common and found in all habitats, particularly shipwrecks.

Redmouth Grouper   *Aethaloperca rogaa*
Size: up to 60 cm (24 in)
Much squarer version of the normal grouper shape. Dark reddish brown to almost black in colour. Has an obvious red mouth when it is open (which is often). Lives in large caverns where it hunts glassfish and hatchetfish. Usually found with Bigeye in the same crevice.

Coral Grouper   *Cephalopholis miniata*
Size: up to 40 cm (16 in)
This is the most strikingly red of all the Red Sea grouper. Covered in dark and light bluish spots, it likes to hang out under table coral and usually with various butterflyfish.

Moon Grouper   *Variola louti*
Size: up to 80 cm (32 in)
Overall red in colour with light and dark bands and numerous spots. Easily identified due to its sickle or lyre tail. Quite common species found in all coral habitats and loves offshore reefs and islands.

Spotted Grouper   *Cephalopholis hemistiktos*
Size: 35cm (14 in)
Mainly red in colour becoming pale towards the base of its tail, which is always a deep, dark reddish brown, fringed in pale blue. More often associated with more open reefs.

Red Stripe Fairy Basslet   *Pseudanthias fasciatus* [endemic]
Size: up to 11 cm (4⅓ in)
Difficult to spot without lights, and rare in the north, as it looks so similar to the other main Red Sea anthias species. Males look almost identical to *A. squamipinnis* but the females have an obvious orangey red stripe along the body.

Red Sea Fairy Basslet *Pseudanthias taeniatus* [endemic]
Size: up to 13 cm (5 in)
Distinctive with its purplish brown body and broad white strip running from just above the eye to its white tail. Always occurring in large numbers and generally mixed in with other anthias species.

Fridman's Dottyback *Pseudochromis fridmani* [endemic]
Size: up to 7 cm (2¾ in)
Spectacularly bright purple in colour, you cannot fail to spot this little dottyback as it flits around the coral recesses and often in large numbers. Surprisingly common, but only described a few years ago.

Gurnard

Helmut Gurnard *Dactyloptena orientalis*
Size: 30 cm (12 in)
The Helmut or Flying gurnard is rare to common, depending on the location. Usually seen in shallow lagoons and along the reef edge. Very distinctive when it takes off and flies over the seabed with its huge brightly coloured wings. Uses adapted ventral fin rays to 'walk' about over the seabed when searching for small molluscs to eat.

Hawkfish

Scalefin Anthias *Anthias squamipinnis*
Size: up to 15 cm (6 in)
The 'goldfish' most synonymous with the entire Red Sea, every reef and particularly every coral wall has simply hundreds of these beautiful fish. Female is golden orange; male turns a lovely lilac to purplish pale brown with a small red marking on the pectoral fin and has a purple/red tail.

Forster's Hawkfish *Paracirrhites forsteri*
Size: 22 cm (8¾ in)
Has a yellowish ochre upper body, white below and the face covered in brownish red spots. Most commonly seen hawkfish, usually perched on coral heads looking for dinner. Easily approached.

Long-nose Hawkfish   *Oxycirrhites typus*
Size: up to 13 cm (5 in)
Being Scottish, I love this fish as it has a 'tartan' design on its skin, of red cross-hatched over white. Also has a distinctive long snout. Almost always found below 18 m (60 ft) where the start of the black coral trees and gorgonian seafans grow, which is their main habitat.

Clearfin Lionfish   *Pterois radiata*
Size: up to 25 cm (10 in)
Smaller than *P. volitans*, rays of its fins are white, much more defined and radiate outwards from a dark reddish brown body with vertical white stripes between the bands.

Pixie Hawkfish   *Cirrhitichthys oxycephalus*
Size: up to 10 cm (4 in)
Has quite a sharp head with a pale grey to silver body, covered in irregular red spots, blotches or bands. Raised dorsal fin rays have very obvious tufts on them. A very shy fish and hides in coral recesses.

Zebra Lionfish   *Dendrochirus zebra*
Size: up to 20 cm (8 in)
Quite rare. Fins are more rounded in shape, but the front dorsal fin rays are quite separate and broad at the top with light and dark bands. Can be quite aggressive if approached too quickly.

Lionfish, Scorpionfish, Stonefish & Crocodilefish

Common Lionfish   *Pterois volitans*
Size: up to 40 cm (16 in)
Mainly reddish brown in colour with alternate stripes of red and white along its spines. Spines on the ends of its dorsal and caudal fins are very poisonous. Now also found in the Caribbean, a voracious predator and is usually found in all types of positions, upside-down in caverns around big schools of Glassy Sweepers.

Shortfin Lionfish   *Dendrochirus brachypterus*
Size: up to 17 cm (6¾ in)
Small scorpionfish with very variable colours from yellow and brown to deep dark red. Its caudal fins are rounded, but the dorsal fin rays are quite broad and separate. Surprisingly common, mostly found in shallow lagoons and near seagrass beds and mangroves.

Flathead Scorpionfish   *Scorpaenopsis oxycephalus*
Size: up to 35 cm (14 in)
Probably the most recognisable of the Red Sea scorpionfish. Usually found on most dives, perched on top of live coral heads, amidst coral rubble or around sponges and soft corals, where it assumes the colour of its background and virtually disappears.

Stonefish   *Synanceia verrucosa*
Size: up to 39 cm (15 in)
Incredibly well camouflaged with a mottled warty appearance of lots of different colours and often algae growing on them due to its sedentary nature. Has an upturned jaw and very venomous spines along the back. Venom is known to be fatal.

Devil Scorpionfish   *Scorpaenopsis diabola*
Size: up to 22 cm (8¾ in)
Drab looking fish with quite a fat, foreshortened head and a raised or humped back. Often covered in detritus, which helps to camouflage it, until it spreads its caudal fins and fantastic colour bands show of reds, oranges and pinks.

Crocodilefish or Carpet Flathead   *Papilloculiceps longiceps*
Size: up to 1 m (40 in)
Very obvious in shape, resembling a crocodile, but like a long thin, flattened scorpionfish with mottled colouring. Found in sand or coral rubble areas or on shipwrecks.

Shortfin Scorpionfish   *Scorpaenodes parvipinnis*
Size: up to 8.5 cm (3⅓ in)
Usually a bright red with white patches and dark markings. Smallest of the scorpionfish. Very shy and usually stays well hidden in coral recesses.

Red Sea Walkman   *Inimicus filamentosus*
Size: up to 25 cm (10 in)
A curious member of the scorpionfish family. Has adapted pectoral fin rays, which it uses to walk over the seabed. Undersides of its fins are very strikingly coloured. Has large eyes on raised stalks to allow it to bury itself in the sand. Dorsal spines are extremely venomous.

Crested Velvetfish   *Ptarmus gallus* [endemic]
Size: 10 cm (4 in)
Brownish, with small paler markings and spotted pectoral fins. Rarely seen in the Red Sea, but more often in the southern region. Resembles the Spiny Waspfish found in the Indo-Pacific. Always motionless on a sandy bottom to assist in its camouflage.

Lizardfish, Sandperch & Stargazer

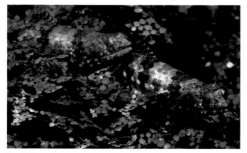

Sand Lizardfish   *Synodus dermatogenys*
Size: 25 cm (10 in)
Very similar to *S. variegatus*, but more likely to be seen in pairs and does like to bury itself in the sand, with only its head and multi-toothed jaw showing. Redder in colour.

Variegated Lizardfish   *Synodus variegatus*
Size: 25 cm (10 in)
More brown or grey with darker blotches along the back and flanks. More often on their own, they sit motionless on the reef and are quite easy to approach.

Speckled Sandperch   *Parapercis hexophthalama*
Size: up to 25 cm (10 in)
Creamy white with reddish brown spots overall and short vertical stripes on either side of the lower head. Usually found motionless on a sandy bottom or amongst coral rubble, where it lies in wait for a likely meal to come along and be snapped up in a lightning-fast movement of its large mouth.

Dollfus' Stargazer   *Uranoscopus dollfusi*
Size: 24 cm (9½ in)
Identified by large black spot on the dorsal fin. Buries itself in the sand and lies in wait with upturned mouth and eyes for a likely prey to swim by, when it lurches upwards, opening its mouth wide and sucking in the prey.

Parrotfish & Wrasses

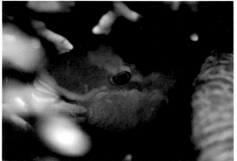

Rusty Parrotfish   *Scarus ferrugineus*
Size: up to 40 cm (16 in)
In shades of green and aquamarine, an active parrotfish, distinguished by its green dental plates.

Bluebarred Parrotfish   *Scarus ghobban*
Size: up to 70 cm (28 in)
Comes in varying shades of blue, aquamarine and green with pink
dental plates. Enjoys all types of habitat including silty lagoons and
even mangrove beds. Can be found readily at night when it builds itself
a protective cocoon to sleep in and deter predators.

Bumphead Parrotfish   *Bolbometopon muricatum*
Size: up to 120 cm (47 in)
Largest of the parrotfish, but extremely rare, generally only found in
the deep south around Rocky Island and the Fury Shoals. Has obvious
bump head. Pale white to greenish colour around the head with
perhaps a pink tinge to the front of the face and around the lips, pulled
back to reveal a huge beak-like jaw.

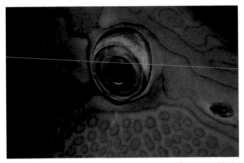

Bicolour Parrotfish   *Cetoscarus bicolor*
Size: up to 90 cm (36 in)
Has very distinctive markings around the face with scrolls of pink
over an aquamarine background. Quite territorial and a male will
have several females in his harem. Widely distributed in all reef and
wreck habitats.

Longnose Parrotfish   *Hipposcarus harid*
Size: up to 75 cm (30 in)
More often seen in large schools along the reef crest, I call this fish the
'Tight-lipped Parrotfish' as its elongated snout and fleshy lips hide the
usual open-beaked physiology of the rest of the Red Sea parrotfish.

Rockmover Wrasse   *Novaculichthys taeniourus*
Size: up to 30 cm (12 in)
Adults and juveniles have totally different colouration. Juvenile's front
two dorsal spines become elongated; very active, and flips and flops
about the reef, like a bit of dead vegetation. Adult is much more
wrasse-like; has dark lines rayed out from the eye, light markings on
each scale and a white band before the tail.

Vermiculate Wrasse   *Macropharyngodon bipartitus*
Size: up to 13 cm (5 in)
Has a huge disparity in colours, but mainly browns and reds. Front of the dorsal fin always faces forwards. Found in lagoons and shallow coral gardens.

Red-breasted Splendour Wrasse   *Cheilinus fasciatus*
Size: up to 38 cm (15 in)
Variable in colour. Has a roundish face, and dark and white vertical bands down its body, but the base colour can be anything from white to orange or brown. Difficult to get close to.

Chiseltooth Wrasse   *Pseudodax moluccanus*
Size: up to 20 cm (8 in)
Has yellow lips, blue markings around the eye, orangey blue markings on the body, and a white band before its dark blue tail. Juveniles resemble cleaner wrasses. Usually found on seaward-facing reefs.

Napoleon Wrasse   *Cheilinus undulatus*
Size: up to 2.3 m (7½ft)
Largest of the wrasses found in the Red Sea. Easily recognised by its large eyes and huge, humped forehead. Greenish in colour with a greeny blue head and scroll-like markings on the face. Adults enjoy outer reef edges and walls.

Ring Wrasse   *Hologymnosus annulatus*
Size: up to 40 cm (16 in)
Much harder to identify as adults, due to the various shades of green shown. Juveniles are obvious with their longitudinal yellow and black stripes that run from the pointed nose to the tail. Juveniles are active in sheltered coral reefs, often in large numbers.

Common Cleaner Wrasse   *Labroides dimidiatus*
Size: up to 11 cm (4⅓ in)
Most common of all the cleaner wrasses in the region and has an obvious pattern of longitudinal stripes, signalling that it is a cleaner.

Arabian Cleaner Wrasse *Larabicus quadrilineatus*
Size: up to 11 cm (4⅓ in)
Seen here cleaning the Masked Puffer of parasites, this little wrasse is distinguished by its blue and black longitudinal lines.

Klunzinger's Wrasse *Thalassoma klunzingeri* [endemic]
Size: up to 20 cm (8 in)
Brightly coloured with pink green, yellow and blue ribbed markings. Abundant on all reef types from inner lagoons to outer reefs such as Elphinstone. Quite aggressive when food is around and will barge in amongst other fish to get its share.

Red Sea Eightline Wrasse *Paracheilinus octotaenia* [endemic]
Size: up to 9 cm (3½ in)
Very colourful with eight mauve stripes over a pinkish body and wide fan-like fins which blend into the tail. Small and difficult to find, but when you do, it is more common than realised.

Bird Wrasse *Gomphosus caeruleus*
Size: up to 30 cm (12 in)
Very distinct velvet blue wrasse with a long bird-like snout for feeding deep in the corals. Has an undulate way of swimming.

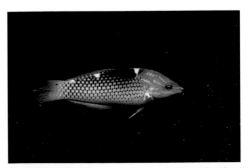

Checkerboard Wrasse *Halichoeres hortulanus*
Size: up to 27 cm (10½ in)
Fantastic colouration with speckles, spots, stripes, splashes of random colour, a yellow tail, black slash below the dorsal fin and radiating pink lines from the eye. Very distinctive.

Clown Coris *Coris aygula*
Size: up to 60 cm (24 in)
Adult is a large blueish green wrasse with a lighter vertical band down its midsection. Juvenile steals the show with a white to pale pink body, black spotted front quarters and two bright orange splashes of colour just below the dorsal fin.

Pufferfish, Boxfish, Filefish, Trunkfish & Sea Moth

Masked Puffer   *Arothron diadematus*
Size: up to 30 cm (12 in)
Most common of all the Red Sea pufferfish. Fairly granular grey in colour with an obvious black mask over the eyes and continuing to the gills. Also has a dark grey nose. Often only found on their own, but in the evenings they congregate in large numbers near the reef crest to mate.

Yellow Boxfish   *Ostracion cubicus*
Size: up to 45 cm (18 in)
Developing various colour stages throughout its life, it starts off as a tiny, yellow square fish with black spots. Gradually becomes more elongated, olive green with blueish spots, then finally, mainly blue in colour with much larger patterns of darker blue spots and a yellow colouration just before its wide tail.

Porcupinefish   *Diodon hystrix*
Size: up to 70 cm (28 in)
An elongated pufferfish, until it decides to inflate if danger threatens. Has large eyes, pale body covered in spots and quite short spines, which stick out and have a dark patch around the base.

Arabian or Blue Boxfish   *Ostracion cyanurus*
Size: up to 15 cm (6 in)
Also goes through several colour transformations. Adult is an overall blue on the sides and belly, and a dark olive green on the flattish back. Sides are also covered in small dark spots. Usually found around patch reefs and shallow lagoons.

Freckled Porcupinefish   *Diodon holocanthus*
Size: up to 30 cm (12 in)
Has very long spines all over the body, which jut out at all angles. Usually solitary on seaward reefs; quite tame and easily approached. Very prone to inflation and should never be handled.

Dwarf Toby *Canthigaster pygmae* [endemic]
Size: up to 6 cm (2½ in)
Has bluish brown, blotched colours and iridescent blue markings around the head. Often rare to see during the day, as it is so small and generally more active at night, however also prone to just sitting on corals and is easily approached.

Seagrass Puffer *Arothron immaculatus*
Size: up to 30 cm (12 in)
More common in the southern Red Sea amongst seagrass beds and fine silty areas. If threatened, simply sinks to the ground and acts like it isn't there!

Whitespotted Puffer *Arothron hispidus*
Size: up to 35 cm (14 in)
Distinguished by the circles around its eyes and the base of its pectoral fins. Mainly found around seagrass beds and shallow marsas.

Scrawled Filefish *Aluterus scriptus*
Size: up to 1 m (40 in)
Elongated and a drab grey/green in colour with very obvious scrawled blue markings all over the face and body, leading to spots just before the tail. Circumtropical. Quite shy and often in pairs.

Giant Puffer *Arothron stellatus*
Size: up to 120 cm (47 in)
Largest of the Red Sea pufferfish. Pale grey in colour and covered in spots. Has a prominent beak. Easy to approach and is just as at home on coral rubble slopes as on seaward-facing coral reefs.

Fuzzy Filefish *Paramonacanthus nematophorus*
Size: up to 9 cm (3½ in)
Small filefish found in all areas of the reef from seagrass beds to colourful soft corals, where it appears to blend in everywhere with its 'fuzzy' skin, high peaked dorsal spine and superb camouflage.

Harlequin Filefish   *Oxymonocanthus halli*
Size: up to 7 cm (2¾ in)
Small, but the most colourful of all the Red Sea filefish. Has a light green body, covered in yellow spots and a dark spot on its tail. Always in mating pairs.

Thornback Trunkfish   *Tetrosomus gibbosus*
Size: up to 30 cm (12 in)
Has a triangular-shaped, leathery body with a high dorsal spike and two forward-facing horns. Markings on the flanks may be honeycomb-shaped. Almost always solitary amidst seagrass beds and coral rubble area.

Sea Moth   *Eurypegasus draconis*
Size: up to 10 cm (4 in)
Wonderfully, curiously shaped and found as far north as Taba and Eilat. Body is covered in knobbly, fused, bony plates. Has a long snout, adapted fin rays to help it walk along the seabed and even little wings to help it coast along faster when searching for food. Spends its whole life on the seabed.

Rabbitfish

Dusky Rabbitfish   *Siganus luridus*
Size: up to 25 cm (10 in)
Dark grey and with irregular black spots. Usually in shallow water and bays, where it may form small groups in the evenings. Easy to approach at night as it falls asleep on the seabed or amongst corals.

Red Sea Rabbitfish   *Siganus rivulatus*
Size: up to 30 cm (12 in)
Pale green to silver in colour. Can be found in schools of a hundred or more, but at night always on its own, pretending to be dead! During the day, they are usually single.

Starry Rabbitfish   *Siganus stellatus*
Size: up to 40 cm (16 in)
Has a greenish-blue body spotted with yellow or brown spots. Often found in association with Coronetfish as they search the reefs for food.

Snapper & Grunt

Dory Snapper   *Lutjanus fulviflamma*
Size: up to 35 cm (14 in)
Silvery with yellow horizontal banding and yellow fins and tail, with an obvious black splotch towards the rear of the body. Usually in fairly large groups and mixed in with goatfish of a similar colour.

Blue-striped Grunt   *Lutjanus kasmira*
Size: up to 35 cm (14 in)
Silver fish changing to yellow towards the rear of the body and tail, with iridescent blue lines along the body. Most common of all the snapper in the Red Sea; usually seen in large schools, mixed in with other snapper, goatfish and even butterflyfish (but usually all of the same colour).

Squirrelfish & Bigeye

Big Lip Snapper   *Lutjanus rivulatus*
Size: up to 80 cm (32 in)
Silvery, with large down-turned, prominent lips. Large snapper forming dense schools of fish along the edge of the reef and just off into deep water. They part just far enough away to let you swim amongst them and are not in the slightest afraid.

White-edged Soldierfish   *Myripristes murdjan*
Size: up to 22 cm (8¾ in)
Silvery red in colour with dark eyes. Has a dark marking at the gill slits. Most common of the squirrelfish; usually forms fairly large groups in caverns and near coral recesses, and often swims well out into the blue when feeding.

Black and White Snapper   *Macolor niger*
Size: up to 60 cm (24 in)
Easy-to-spot large snapper; smoky grey and black in colour. Name comes from the juveniles which have very obvious black and white markings. Usually forms fairly large schools in open water.

Bloodspot Squirrelfish   *Neoniphon sammara*
Size: up to 24 cm (9½ in)
Angular fish with metallic silver and brownish red stripes. Lower body blue changing to a yellowish upper body and yellow markings on the tail. Usually in protected bays and lagoons. Active night feeder and always better observed in the evening, as they leave the reef.

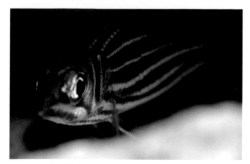

Crown Squirrelfish *Sargocentron diadema*
Size: 17 cm (6¾ in)
Has obvious colouration with a red body and head, and horizontal strips all along its back and body. Usually found on its own.

Common Bigeye *Priacanthus hamrur*
Size: up to 40 cm (16 in)
Overall red in colour. Always found on the outer reef and often in fairly large numbers. Very obvious fish to see on the reef.

White-tail Squirrelfish *Sargocentron caudimaculatum*
Size: 25 cm (10 in)
Another obvious small squirrelfish with a red body fading down to a pure white tail. Tail is only visible during the day, as it turns dark at night when they are out feeding.

Bloch's Bigeye *Priacanthus blochii*
Size: up to 30 cm (12 in)
Very similar to *P. hamrur*, but has a more blotched, silvery red colour. Solely nocturnal and only seen during night dives.

Surgeonfish, Unicornfish & Tangs

Giant Squirrelfish *Sargocentron spiniferum*
Size: up to 45 cm (18 in)
Largest of the squirrelfish in the Red Sea. Has a large high body and its preopercular spine (just below the gill flap) is poisonous. Nocturnal, but easily observed in caves and caverns during the day.

Arabian Surgeonfish or Sohal *Acanthurus sohal*
Size: 40 cm (16 in)
Distinctive surgeonfish with black fins and tail, many lateral stripes, and a yellow splash behind the caudal fin and on the 'blade' just before the tail. Common in the surf zone at the crest of the reef and on shipwrecks.

Shortnose Unicornfish *Naso unicornis*
Size: up to 70 cm (28 in)
Distinguished by its short 'unicorn' spike directly in front of its eyes. Generally a grey to olive green in colour, has blue flashes on the two sets of 'blades' just before the tail. Often seen in fairly large groups amongst other schools of fish off Ras Muhammed.

Sailfin Tang *Zebrasoma desjardinii*
Size: up to 40 cm (16 in)
Quite disc-like in shape. Has vertical yellowish bands and spots, and a spotted tail and head over a dark grey/green body. Generally in pairs on the open reef and usually with other species of tang and butterflyfish.

Sweepers, Emperors & Sweetlips

Orangespine Unicornfish *Naso lituratus*
Size: up to 50 cm (20 in)
Uniform dark slate grey in colour with a yellowish fringe to the dorsal fin and brilliant yellow markings on the two sets of blades before the tail. Appears to prefer reef crests, shipwrecks and most open reefs.

Black-spotted Sweetlips *Plectorhinchus gaterinus*
Size: up to 45 cm (18 in)
Most common of the sweetlips in the Red Sea. Has obvious dark spots over all of its silvery body; brilliant yellow lips, fins and tail. Usually forms small groups under table corals, or very large aggregations on the open reef.

Yellowtail Tang *Zebrasoma xanthurum*
Size: up to 25 cm (10 in)
Very distinctive with its purple/blue body and yellow tail. Enjoys its own company as well as forming large groups in the evenings on the reef crest.

Striped Sweetlips *Plectorhinchus albavittatus*
Size: up to 50 cm (20 in)
Not as common as *P. gaterinus*, this species has longitudinal stripes over all of its blue body, and yellow face and fins.

Dusky Sweeper or Hatchetfish   *Pempheris odusta*
Size: up to 17 cm (6¾ in)
Forms small moving schools; loves overhanging ledges, small caverns and crevices where it shelters during daylight hours, before leaving the reef at night to feed.

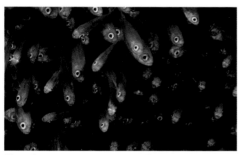

Glassy Sweepers   *Parapriacanthus ransonneti*
Size: up to 10 cm (4 in)
Translucent to olive green in colour. Very common in all locations of the Red Sea, wherever there is a cavern in the coral. Forms huge schools whilst amongst the reef and is actively predated upon by lionfish, grouper and trevally of all kinds. Disperses at night to feed on plankton in the open sea.

Bigeye Emperor   *Monotaxis grandoculis*
Size: up to 60 cm (24 in)
Has a fairly round, silvery body with yellow markings around the eye and pinkish caudal fins. Fairly common outside all reefs, where it can form large irregular schools, particularly off Ras Muhammed during the summer months.

Trevally (Jacks) & Fusiliers

Bigeye Trevally   *Caranx sexfasciatus*
Size: up to 80 cm (32 in)
Silvery blue fish with strong lines leading to the forked tail. By far the most common trevally on the Red Sea reefs. When not hunting in small packs around the reefs, they form large schools just off the reef wall.

Goldbody Trevally   *Carangoides bajad*
Size: up to 55 cm (22 in)
Can be completely golden, or silver with gold spots. Usually mixes in with other trevally, and even goatfish and snapper when swimming close to the reef.

Bluebar Trevally   *Carangoides ferdau*
Size: up to 70 cm (28 in)
Has a more rounded face and dark blue vertical bands down the body. Usually in small schools and often mixed in with other trevally. Always fairly close to the reef edge, where they feed on Glassy Sweepers and other small fish.

Bluefin Trevally   *Caranx melampygus*
Size: up to 1 m (40 in)
Has a yellow tinge to the upper body, and very obvious blue fins and
tail; the body is covered in small blue dots. Common in large schools
around Ras Muhammed and around most seaward reefs, where they
hunt in small groups.

Golden Pilot Jack   *Gnathodon speciosus*
Size: up to 110 cm (44 in)
Juvenile has a distinctive, golden yellow body with black vertical
bands. Adult loses this banded colouration and becomes a more
uniform silver grey in colour with a yellow tinge and occasional black
spots along its flanks. Juveniles always accompany large creatures,
such as sharks, Whale Sharks, turtles and Dugong.

Pilotfish   *Naucrates ductor*
Size: up to 70 cm (28 in)
Has a silvery grey body with dark blue/black vertical lines. Usually
seen accompanying Oceanic Whitetip Sharks around Elphinstone and
Daedalus reefs. Is very much at home accompanying larger hosts,
where it cleans off their parasites and eats any left-over food scraps.

Yellowstripe Scad   *Selaroides leptolepis*
Size: up to 22 cm (8¾ in)
Distinctive yellow stripe is very obvious. Rare in the northern Red Sea,
but often seen in the south in fairly large schools. Swims fairly close to
the edge of the outer reefs.

Red Sea Fusilier   *Caesio suevica* [endemic]
Size: up to 25 cm (10 in)
Distinguished by the black blotch at the caudal fin, and white and
black tips to its tail. Swift and slender; always has hundreds of friends
around it.

Triggerfish

Titan Triggerfish *Balistoides viridescens*
Size: up to 75 cm (30 in)
Overall olive green in colour with darker markings on each large scale, and equal sized dorsal and anal fins. Probably the most aggressive of all the triggerfish. Guards its nest on shallow open sandy or coral rubble areas in lagoons and will attack anything or anyone that comes near it. May follow divers for quite some time and can cause serious injury if not heeded.

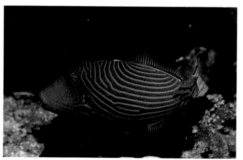

Orange-striped Triggerfish *Balistopus undulatus*
Size: up to 30 cm (12 in)
Has a green body with diagonal golden stripes and golden spots around the snout. With its stout jaws, it feeds on molluscs and clams. Quite a common triggerfish amidst the corals and sponges on all reefs.

Blue Triggerfish *Pseudobalistes fuscus*
Size: up to 40 cm (16 in)
Overall dark blue in colour with a paler blue fringe to the fins and tail, and scroll-like markings around the face. Often found in large numbers in the evenings swimming around the reef crest; more usually on its own around most seaward-facing coral reefs.

Picasso Triggerfish *Rhinecanthus assasi*
Size: up to 30 cm (12 in)
Beautiful triggerfish with unmistakable markings and well named! Very busy on the reef and usually on its own.

Bluethroat Triggerfish *Sufflamen albicaudatus*
Size: up to 18 cm (7 in)
Has a distinctive blue throat and lips, and an almost vertical pale blue line from under the eye to the base of the fish. Has lovely tail markings. Rarely seen in the north, but only because it is so shy, it quickly hides in the reef as you approach it.

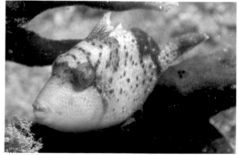

Yellowmargin Triggerfish *Pseudobalistes flavimarginatus*
Size: up to 60 cm (24 in)
Wide ranging in the Red Sea and often confused with the Titan Triggerfish (above). Found singly or in pairs in shallow lagoons and sheltered reef areas. Juvenile pictured.

Glossary

Antennae Projecting feelers which are sensory.

Appendage Part of an organism that projects from the body and has a specific function.

Benthos/Benthic The seabed and animals/plants that live there.

Carapace The hard upper or outer shell of a turtle or crustacean.

Cerata The fleshy extensions on the back on a nudibranch which often store toxins from their prey to help in their own defence.

Chelipeds A crustacean's claws.

Circumtropical Found in all tropical oceans of the world.

Coralline Resembles the material from calcareaous coral skeletons.

Caudal As in caudal fin, the tail.

Demersal Living and feeding on or near the bottom of seas or lakes.

Detritus Particulates of algae and animal matter, which can become attached to the spines of various crustaceans and fish.

Dorsal As in dorsal fin, which is the fin on the top of the back.

Mantle The fold of skin that extends from the body of a mollusc, such as a cowrie, and completely covers the outer shell.

Medusa The free-swimming stage of jellyfish where they most resemble an anemone or coral polyp.

Nematocyst The harpoon-like spike which is fired from certain invertebrates in defence or to stun prey for food.

Operculum The hard bony plate that acts as a protective plate to the gills of a bony fish.

Orbicular Round or oval shaped.

Panglobal Found in every ocean of the world.

Pantropical Found between the Tropics of Cancer and Capricorn around the world.

Papillae Sensory extrusions on the mantle of a cowrie (for instance).

Pectoral As in pectoral fin, found on the sides of a fish, usually behind the gills.

Polyp Either six- or eight-armed, anemone-shaped depending on the species genus.

Radula The grinding plates in certain fish and nudibranchs to aid digestion.

Rhinophores The sensory appendages on the head of nudibranchs.

Rostrum Beak-like projection.

Scutes The horny plates that form the shell of turtles.

Test Shell or body.

Spicules Calcium spikes found in sponges and soft corals.

Ventral As in ventral or pelvic fin, found on the bottom of fish.

Useful Contacts and Further Reading

Fish Base, a global database of fish species: www.fishbase.org
Hurghada Environmental Protection and Conservation Association: www.hepca.org
Marine Conservation Society: www.mcs.org
Marine Biological Conservation Society: www.marinebio.org
World Register of Marine Species (WORMS): www.marinespecies.org

Diving and Tourism

Aggressor Fleet International: www.aggressor.com
Aqua Sport International: www.aqua-sport.com
Blue 'O' Two: www.blueotwo.com
Blue Planet Live-aboards: www.blueplanet-liveaboards.com
Camel Dive Club: www.cameldive.com
Deep Blue Adventures: www.deepblueadventures.com
Dive In Dahab: www.diveindahab.com
Dive Quest: www.divequest-diving-holidays.co.uk
Divernet: www.divernet.com
Dive World Wide: www.diveworldwide.com
Dive The World: www.dive-world-wide.com
Diverse Travel: www.diversetravel.co.uk
Eagle Divers: www.eagle-divers.com
Emperor Divers: www.emperordivers.com
Holiday Designers: www.holiday-designers.com
Lahami Bay: www.lahamibay.com
Live Aboard Holidays: www.liveaboard.com
Ocean College: www.ocean-college.com
Oonas Dive Club: www.oonasdiveclub.com
Pharohs Dive Clubs: www.pharohdiveclubs.com
Planet Diving: www.planetdiveholidays.com
Red Sea Diving College: www.redseacollege.com
Red Sea Holidays: www.redseaholidays.com
Red Sea Scuba: ww.redseascuba-intl.com
Red Sea Waterworld: www.redseawaterworld.com
Reef 2000: www.reef2000.com
Regal Diving: www.regal-dive.com
Sea Queen Fleet: www.seaqueens.com
Sinai College: www.sinai-college.com
Sinai Divers: www.sinaidivers.com
Thomson Holidays: www.thomson.co.uk

Werner Lau Dive Centre: www.wernerlau.com

X Ray Magazine: ww.xray-mag.com

www.touregypt.net

www.gotoegypt.org

www.egyptianconsulate.co.uk

Books

Bergbauer, M. & Kirshner, M. (2011). *Diving & Snorkelling Guide to Tropical Marine Life of the Indo-Pacific Region*. John Beaufoy Publishing

Humann, P. & Deloach, N. (2010). *Reef Creature Identification, Tropical Pacific*. New World Publications.

Allen, G., Steene, R., Humann, P. & Deloach, N. (2015). *Reef Fish Identification, Tropical Pacific*. New World Publications.

Middleton, N. (2010). *Shipwrecks from the Egyptian Red Sea*. Ashgrove Publishing.

(2012). *The Official HEPCA Red Sea Dive Guide*. Hurghada Environmental Protection and Conservation Association.

Wood, L. (2012). *The World's Best Tropical Dive Destinations*. John Beaufoy Publishing.

Debelius, H. (1993). *Indian Ocean Tropical Fish Guide*. Aquaprint Verlags GmbH.

Debelius, H. (2013). *Indian Ocean Reef Guide*. Conch Books.

Debelius, H. (2000). *Red Sea Reef Guide*. Circle Publishing.

Debelius, H. & Kuiter, R. H. (2007). *Nudibranchs of the World*. IKAN Unterwasser-Archiv.

Acknowledgements

This book would not have possible without the support of my wife Lesley who is always there by my side. Luke Atkinson and Emperor Divers have been incredibly helpful and professional. Luke is an excellent underwater photographer and I have great pleasure in including a few of his photographs in this book as a big 'thank you'. Alain Sobol from the Red Sea Diving College, whom I have been friends with for over 30 years; my great friend Claude Antoine and his Teknical Department; Petra & Rolph Schmidt from Sinai Divers and Hesham Gabr from Camel Divers have been close friends since the early 1980's and I have relied on them to supply the most up-to-date information about the southern Sinai Peninsula. The *VIP ONE* live-aboard dive boat was used for a number of my trips and countless day boats also from Emperor Divers. Ned Middleton, whose book on the Red Sea Shipwrecks is a superb resource; Dan Lyon of Holiday Designers; Blue O Two; Oonasdivers; Regal Diving; Scuba Travel; Jim Yanny; Steve & Miranda Coverdale; Peter Collings; Tony Turner and Red Sea Adventures and the amazing *Lady Jenny III* and *Lady Jenny V*; Bob Evans; Paul Duxfield; Reeta and James Tunney.

I would like to also pay tribute to the Sinai Survivors, my close group of friends who became part of my family when I worked in the Red Sea between 1982 and 1986 aboard the legendary *Lady Jenny III* and *Lady Jenny V*. We survived storm, tempest, injuries beyond belief and almost sinking; witnessed ships being wrecked; discovered the identity of shipwrecks; and experienced some of the best diving and exploring of the Red Sea.

Index

Abu Dabab 82
Abudefduf sexfasciatus 128
Abudefduf vaigensis 128
Abu Galawa Kebir 71
Abu Galawa Soraya 70
Abu Ghoson 83
Abu Kizan 69
Acabaria pulchra 93
Acabaria splendens 92
Acanthaster planci 27, 29, 36, 98
Acanthophiotrix purpurea 99
Acanthurus sohal 148
Acheus spinosus 109
Acropora granulosa 94
Acropora hemprichii 95
Acropora latistella 94
Acropora paniculata 94
Aeoliscus strigatus 130
Aethaloperca rogaa 136
Aetobatus narinari 118
Alicia mirabilis 97
Alopias vulpinus 36, 120
Alpheus bellulus 113
Alpheus ochrostriatus 113
Alpheus rubromaculatus 113
Aluterus scriptus 145
Amblyeleotris steinitzi 26, 134
Amblyglyphodon flavilatus 128
Amblyglyphodon indicus 128
Amblygobius albimaculatus 134
Amphiprion bicinctus 27, 126
Anemone, Adhesive 97
    Burrowing Tube 96
    Carrier 97
    Magnificent 96
    Ribbed 97
Anemonefish 27, 46, 96, 126, 127
Anemonefish, Red Sea 46, 96, 126, 127
Anemones 96, 140
Angelfish 53, 80, 119, 120, 121
Angelfish, Arabian 121
    Blue 121
    Emperor 53, 121
    Lyretail 80, 121
    Regal 120
Anglerfish, Shaggy 132
Anilocra spp. 114
Annella mollis 93
Antipathes dichotoma 92
Antennarius coccineus 132
Antennarius commersoni 132
Antennarius hispidus 132
Antennarius pictus 132
Anthias squamipinnis 137
Anthias, Scalefin 137
Antipathes dichotoma 92
Apogon fraenatus 125
Apogon urostigma 125
Archamia fucata 126
Arothron diadematus 144
Arothron hispidus 145

Arothron immaculatus 145
Arothron stellatus 145
Aseraggodes melanostictus 130
Asthenosoma marisrubri 99
Astroba nuda 99
Auger, Marlinspike 107
    Subulate 107
Aurelia aurita 90
Bab el-Mandeb Strait 8, 22
Balistoides viridescens 152
Balistopus undulatus 152
Bannerfish, Red Sea 124
    Schooling 80, 124
Barracuda 121, 122
Barracuda, Blackfin 121
    Great 122
Basslet, Red Sea Fairy 137
    Red Stripe Fairy 136
Batfish 122
Batfish, Circular 122
    Longfin 122
Beacon Rock 61
Big Brother Island 20, 65
Bigeye 66, 136, 147, 148, 150
Bigeye, Bloch's 148
    Common 148
Bispira spp. 101
Blenny, Black-lined Fang 122
    Blue-striped Sabre-toothed 123
    Chestnut 123
    Gorgonian 133
    Leopard 123
    Red Sea Combtooth 123
    Red Sea Mimic 122
    Scale-eating Sabretooth 122
Blennies 122
Blind Reef Sha'b El Erg 64
Bohadschia graeffei 100
Bolbometopon muricatum 141
Bothus pantherinus 130
Boxfish 144
Boxfish, Yellow 144
Bryanopsis tigris 133
Bryanopsis yongei 26, 28, 134
Butterflyfish 68, 77, 82, 117, 123, 124, 125
Butterflyfish, Black-backed 124
    Chevron 125
    Lined 124
    Masked 82, 124
    Orangehead 125
    Polyp 123
    Red-backed 125
    Striped 77, 123
    Threadfin 125
    Yellow Longnose 124
Caesio suevica 151
Calcinus rosaceus 110
Callyactis polypus 97
Calpurnus verrucosus 107
Candelabra, Purple 92

Canthigaster pygmae 145
Carangoides bajad 150
Carangoides ferdau 150
Caranx melampygus 151
Caranx sexfasciatus 150
Carcharhinus albimarginatus 120
Carcharhinus falciformis 120
Carcharhinus limbatus 119
Carcharhinus longimanus 36, 119
Cardinalfish 125, 126
Cardinalfish, Fiveline 126
    Iridescent 125
    Orange-lined 126
    Spinyhead 125
Caretta caretta 115
Carpilius convexus 109
Carrier, Sponge 108
Cassiopea andromeda 90
Catfish, Striped Eel 128
Cedar Pride 15
Cephalopholis miniata 136
Ceratosoma tenue 103
Ceratosoma, Purple-edged 103
Cerianthus spp. 96
Cetoscarus bicolor 141
Chaetodon auriga 125
Chaetodon austriacus 123
Chaetodon fasciatus 123
Chaetodon larvatus 125
Chaetodon lineolatus 124
Chaetodon melannotus 124
Chaetodon paucifasciatus 125
Chaetodon semilarvatus 124
Chaetodon trifascialis 125
Cheilinus fasciatus 142
Cheilinus undulatus 142
Cheilodipterus quinquelineatus 126
Chelidonura, Red Sea 102
Chelonia mydas 48, 115
Chloea flava 102
Chromis 126, 127
Chromis dimidiata 127
Chromis viridis 127
Chromodoris geminus 103
Chromodoris quadricolor 104
Chromodoris, Twin 103
Cinetorhynchus hendersoni 111
Cinetorhynchus reticulatus 111
Cirrhipathes spiralis 92
Cirrhitichthys oxycephalus 138
Cirripectes castaneus 123
Clam, Fire 105
    Squamose Giant 105
Clanculus pharaoensis 106
Cleaning stations 24
Clingfish 130
Clingfish, Striped 130
Cnidarians 36
Commensalism 25
Cone, Textile 106
Cone Shell, Map 106

Sand Dusted 106
Conus cinereus 129
Conus geographus 106
Conus tessulatus 106
Conus textile 106
Copepod, Parasitic 114
Copepods 114
Coral Island 15, 47, 76
Coral Tree, Black 92
    Midnight Cup 94
Coral, Bristle 96
    Broccoli 91
    Bubble 94, 113
    Common Mushroom 96
    Common Toadstool 91
    Cone 95
    Elephant Skin 95
    Fuzzy Spiral Table 94
    Golden Cup 94
    Granular Table 94
    Hickson's Fan 93
    Klunzinger's Soft 91
    Net Fire 89
    Organ Pipe 93
    Plate Fire 89
    Scuted Mushroom 96
    Secret 95
    Spiny Row 96
    Spiral Wire 92
    Splendid Knotted Fan 92
    Staghorn 95
    Stony 95
    Uniform Brain 95
    Vibrant Soft 91
    Yellow Waver 93
Corals 69, 91, 93, 95
Corals, Hard 93
Corals, Leathery 91
Corals, Soft 91
Coral Shrimpfish 130
Coris, Clown 143
Coris aygula 143
Coronetfish 126, 146
Corythoichthys flavofasciatus 131
Corythoichthys nigripectus 131
Corythoichthys schultzi 131
Cotylorhiza tuberculata 90
Cowrie, Egg 107
    Exusta 108
    False 107
    Gray's Arabica 108
    Lynx 108
    Mole 107
    Talpa 107
Crab, Coral 108, 109
    Coral Spider 109
    Crinoid 109
    Porcelain 27, 28
    Red-spotted Porcelain 27
    Soft Coral Spider 109
    Spiny Spider 109
    Splendid Coral 108
    Sponge 108
Variable Coral 109
Crabs 108, 110

Crenimugil crenibalis 133
Crocodilefish 138, 139
Crustaceans 108
Cryptodendrum adhaesivum 97
Cucumber, Flower 100
    Tubercle Sea 100
Cuttlefish, Hooded 104
Cymodacea cerulatta 18
Cymodacea rotundata 18
Dactyloptena orientalis 137
Daedalus 12, 69, 119, 151
Dahab 50, 77
Damsel, Lemon 127
Damselfish 115, 126, 127, 128
Damselfish, Jewel 127
    Pale 128
    Yellowside 128
Dardanus lagopodes 110
Dardanus pedunculatus 110
Dardanus tinctor 97, 110
Dascyllus, Arabian 126
    Three-spot 49, 96, 127
Dascyllus marginatus 126
Dascyllus trimaculatus 127
Dashret 10
Dasycaris zanzibarica 111
Dendrochirus brachypterus 138
Dendrochirus zebra 138
Dendronephthya hemprichi 91
Dendronephthya klunzingeri 10, 91
Diadema paucispinum 27, 100
Diademichthys lineatus 130
Diodogorgia nodulifera 93
Diodon holocanthus 144
Diodon hystrix 144
Dolphin, Bottlenose 116
    Spinner 116
Dolphins 61, 62, 64, 67, 71, 84, 116
Dottyback, Fridman's 137
Dragonfish, Little 28
Dromidiopsis dubia 108
Dugong 18, 22, 82, 88, 115, 117, 133, 151
Dugong dugon 117
Dunkerocampus boylei 131
Echidna nebulosa 129
Echineus naucrates 133
Echinometra mathaei 100
Eel, Garden 128
    Moustached Conger 129
Eels 118, 128
El Gourna 64
Elisus splendidus 108
Ellisella juncea 92
Elphinstone 12, 19, 68, 69, 71, 119, 120, 143, 151
Emperor, Bigeye 150
Emperors 133, 149
Epinephelus fasciatus 135
Epinephelus polyphekadion 135
Epinephelus tauvina 135
Eretmochelys imbricata 115
Escenius dentex 123
Escenius gravieri 122
Eurypegasus draconis 28, 146
Exallias brevis 123

Family Cymodocea 88
Fan, Fragile Yellow Net 92
    Red Crest Fragile Net 93
Favites abdita 95
Feather Hydroid, Stinging 89
Feather Star, Palm-frond 98
Filefish 144, 145, 146
Filefish, Fuzzy 145
    Harlequin 146
    Scrawled 145
Fistularia commersonii 126
Flathead, Carpet 139
Flatworm, Tiger 102
Flounder 130
Flounder, Leopard 130
Forcipiger flavissimus 124
Foul Bay 72
Frogfish 130, 132
Frogfish, Freckled 132
    Giant 132
    Painted 132
    Sargassum 132
Fromia monilis 97
Fromia nodosa 97
Fungia fungites 96
Fungia scutaria 96
Funiculina spp 101
Fury Shoals 70, 71, 73, 84, 116, 132, 141
Fusilier, Red Sea 151
Fusiliers 150
Galathea balssi 110
Galaxea fascicularis 96
Galeocerdo cuvier 119
Genicanthus caudovittatus 121
Gnathodon speciosus 151
Goatfish 77, 127, 133
Goatfish, Red Sea 133
    Yellowfin 77, 133
    Yellowsaddle 133
Gobies 59, 133
Gobiodon citrinus 134
Goby, Blackfin Dart 135
    Citron 134
    Michel's Host 134
    Orange-dashed 134
    Red Fire 135
    Shrimp 26
    Tailspot 134
    Whip Coral 26, 134
Gomphosus caeruleus 143
Gorgasia sillneri 128
Great Rift Valley 8, 20
Green Chromis 127
Grouper 78, 135, 136
Grouper, Blacktip 135
    Coral 78, 136
    Greasy 135
    Marbled 135
    Moon 136
    Redmouth 136
    Spotted 136
Grunt 147
Grunt, Blue-striped 147
Gulf of Aqaba 8, 15, 31, 47
Gurnard 137

Gurnard, Helmut 137
Gymnothorax javanicus 130
Gymnothorax nudivomer 129
Gymnothorax undulatus 129
Halichoeres hortulanus 143
Halodula uninervis 18
Halophila ovalis 18
Halophila stipulacea 18
Hamata 45, 68, 69, 70, 71, 73, 84
Hatchetfish 47, 150
Hawkfish 47, 53, 72, 80, 92, 137, 138
Hawkfish, Forster's 80, 137
   Long-nose 47, 53, 72, 138
   Pixie 138
Heniochus diphreutes 124
Heniochus intermedius 124
Hermit Crab, Anemone 110
   Common 110
   Rosy 110
   White-stalked 110
Hermit Crabs 110
Heteractis aurora 97
Heterocentrotus mammillatus 100
Heterometra savigny 99
Heteroxenia fuscescen 91
Hexabranchus sanguineus 26, 104
Hippocampus fuscus 132
Hipposcarus harid 141
Histrio histrio 132
Hoplophrys oatesii 109
Hurghada 14, 18, 19, 20, 43, 45, 64
Hyastenus spp. 109
Hydnophora exesa 95
Hydroids 89
Hymenocera picta 111
Hyperbaric chamber 35
Inimicus filamentosus 28, 139
Jack, Golden Pilot 151
Jellyfish 36, 90
Jellyfish, Crown 90
   Moon 90
   Upside-down 90
Labroides dimidiatus 24, 25, 123, 142
Lampometra klunzingeri 98
Larabicus quadrilineatus 143
Leptoria phrygia 95
Lima vulgaris 105
Lincina lynx 108
Linckia multiflora 98
Linkia laevigata 98
Lionfish 35, 138
Lionfish, Clearfin 138
   Shortfin 138
   Zebra 138
   Common 138
Lithophytum arboreum 91
Little Brother Island 65, 120
Lizardfish 140
Lizardfish, Sand 140
   Variegated 140
Lobster, Common Spiny 114
   Painted Spiny 114
   Slipper 114
   Soft Coral Squat 110
Lobsters & Shrimps 110

Lopha cristagalli 105
Lutjanus fulviflamma 147
Lutjanus kasmira 147
Lutjanus rivulatus 147
Lysmata amboinensis 112
Macolor niger 147
Macropharyngodon bipartitus 142
Macrorhynchia philippina 89
Manta birostris 119
Manta Point 64
Marine Conservation 30
Marsa Agla 82
Marsa Alam 14, 18, 19, 43, 45, 66, 67, 68, 69, 82, 83, 115, 117, 134
Marsa Bareika 58
Marsa Luli 82
Marsa Malek 82
Marsa Morena 66, 82
Marsa Mubarak 82
Marsa Souni Kebir 66, 82
Marsupenaeus japonicus 111
Mauritia grayana 108
Meicanthus nigrolineatus 122
Mesocentrotus francisanus 36
Metapenaeopsis aegyptica 111
Microcyphus rousseaui 100
Millepora dichotoma 89
Millepora platyphylla 89
Mimicry 25
Mitre, Reticulate 107
Molluscs 103
Monotaxis grandoculis 150
Moray Eel, Undulated 129
   White-eyed 129
Moray Eels 118
Moray, Giant 130
   Peppered 129
   Snowflake 129
   Yellowmouth 129
Moses Rock 46
Moth, Sea 28, 46, 48, 144, 146
Mullet 133
Mullet, Fringe-lip 133
Mulloides vanicolensis 133
Muraenidae 118
Mutualism 26
Myripristes murdjan 147
Myzostomatidae spp. 102
Na'ama Bay 42, 51, 52, 55, 78, 79, 130
Naso lituratus 149
Naso unicornis 149
Naucrates ductor 151
Nebrius ferrugineus 119
Needlefish 77, 126
Negombata corticata 88
Nemateleotris magnifica 135
Paramonacanthus nematophorus 145
Neoniphon sammara 147
Neopetrolisthes maculatus 27, 28
Novaculichthys taeniourus 25, 141
Nudibranch, Pyjama 88, 104
   Serpent 104
   Tubastrea-eating 103
Nudibranchs 103
Nuweiba 15, 48, 49

Octopus 104
Octopus, Reef 104
Octopus cayaneus 104
Oligometra serripinna 98
Olive, Red Mouth 106
Oliva miniacea 106
Ophiothrix savignyi 99
Ostracion cubicus 144
Ostracion cyanurus 144
Ovula ovum 107
Ovula, Umbilical 107
Oxycirrhites typus 138
Oxymonocanthus halli 146
Oyster, Cock's Comb 105
   Red Sea Thorny 105
   Winged 105
Pachyceris speciosa 95
Painted Lady 112
Panulirus penicillatus 114
Panulirus versicolor 114
Papilloculiceps longiceps 139
Paracheilinus octotaenia 143
Paracirrhites forsteri 137
Paramonacanthus nematophorus 145
Parapeneus forsskali 133
Parapercis hexophthalama 140
Parapriacanthus guentheri 23
Parapriacanthus ransonneti 150
Parrotfish & Wrasse 140
Parrotfish, Bicolour 141
   Bluebarred 141
   Bumphead 85, 141
   Longnose 141
   Rusty 140
Parupeneus cyclostomus 133
Pastinachus sephen 118
Pavona claevis 95
Pedum spondyloideum 106
Pempheris odusta 150
Penneatula spp. 101
Pereclimenes imperator 26, 27, 28
Periclimenes brevicarpalis 113
Periclimenes imperator 104, 112
Periclimenes lanipes 112
Periclimenes soror 112
Pharaoh's Island 47, 76
Phestilla melanobranchia 103
Photoblepharon 27
Phylidiella pustulosa 103
Phyllidia varicosa 103
Phylum Cnidaria 89
Pilotfish 151
Pipefish 28, 51, 61, 67, 130, 131, 143
Pipefish, Black-breasted 131
   Network 131
   Ornate Ghost 28, 51, 61, 130
   Ringed 131
   Robust Ghost 28, 67, 131
   Schultz's 131
   Slender 131
Plagiotremus rhinorhynchus 123
Plagiotremus tapeinosoma 122
Platax orbicularis 122
Platax teira 122
Plectorhinchus albavittatus 149

Plectroglyphidodon lacrymatus 127
Plectropomus pessuliferus marisrubri 136
Pleurobranch, Large 102
Pleurobranchus grandis 102
Pleurogyra synplex 94
Pleurosicya micheli 134
Plotosus lineatus 128
Pomacanthus imperator 121
Pomacanthus maculosus 121
Pontonoides unciger 110, 111
Porcupinefish 125, 144
Porcupinefish, Freckled 144
Port Ghalib 66, 69, 70, 73, 82
Prawn, Egyptian 111
    Japanese Sand 111
Priacanthus blochii 148
Priacanthus hamrur 148
Pseudanthias fasciatus 136
*Pseudobalistes flavimarginatusi*152
Pseudanthias taeniatus 137
Pseudobalistes fuscus 152
Pseudoceros dimidiatus 102
Pseudochromis fridmani 137
Pseudodax moluccanus 142
Pseudopterogorgia bipinnata 92
Pseudorca crassidens 117
Ptarmus gallus 140
Pteraeolidia ianthina 104
Ptereleotris evides 135
Pteria aegyptiaca 105
Pterois radiata 138
Pterois volitans 35, 138
Puffer, Giant 77, 145
    Masked 143, 144
    Seagrass 145
    Whitespotted 145
Pufferfish 144
Puller, Bicolor 127
    Blue-green 127
Pycnogonid spp. 114
Pygoplites diacanthus 120
Rabbitfish 146
Rabbitfish, Dusky 146
    Red Sea 146
    Starry 146
Ras Abu Galum 48, 49
Ras Mamlach 48
Ras Muhammed Marine National Park 31, 59, 81
Ras Nasrani 78
Ras Umm Sid 20, 52, 53, 79, 93
Ras Zatar 20, 58, 120
Ray, Eagle 118
    Scalloped Torpedo 118
    Manta 119
Reef, Carless 64
    Dolphin 67
    Gordon 53, 54, 80
    Jackson 20, 55, 56, 57, 80, 119, 121
    Maxwell's 46
    St John's 73, 85
    Thomas 53, 55
    Woodhouse 20, 56, 57
Remora 133

Remora, Striped 133
Rhincodon typus 120
Rhinecanthus assasi 152
Rhynchodon typus 22
Resbecia, Cute 104
Risbecia pulchella 104
Rocky Island 70, 72, 73, 141
Sabellastarte indica 101
Sabellastarte sanctijosephi 101
Sabellastarte spectabilis 101
Sanafir 19, 31, 117
Sandperch 140
Sandperch, Speckled 140
Sarcophyton trocheliophorum 91
Sargocentron caudimaculatum 148
Sargocentron diadema 148
Sargocentron spiniferum 148
Saron marmoratus 112
Scabricola fissurata 107
Scad, Yellowstripe 151
Scallop, Coral 106
Scarus ferrugineus 140
Scarus ghobban 141
Scorpaenodes parvipinnis 139
Scorpaenopsis diabola 139
Scorpaenopsis oxycephalus 139
Scorpionfish 138, 139, 141
Scorpionfish, Devil 139
    Flathead 139
    Shortfin 139
Scyllarides tridacnophaga 114
Sea Cucumbers 100
Sea Pen, Bushy 101
    Tall 101
Sea Pens 101
Sea Star, Blue 98
    Multipore 98
    Pearl 97
    Tile 97
Seafan, Giant 93, 59, 62, 63, 64, 79, 138, 150
    Purple Dwarf Gorgonian 93
Seafans 92, 108
Seagrass 18, 88, 145
Seahorse, Spotted 132
Seahorses 130
Sea Spider 114
Sea Urchins 27, 76, 99
Seawhip, Cluster 92
Sea Whips 92
Sea Worms 101
Selaroides leptolepis 151
Sepia prashdi 104
Sepioteuthis lessoniana 105
Sergeant Major, Indo-Pacific 128
    Scissortail 128
Seriatopora hystrix 96
Sha'ab Abu Nuhas 19, 43, 64
Sha'ab Ali 19, 22, 60, 61
Sha'ab El Erg 63, 64
Sha'ab Samadai 67
Sha'ab Sataya 84
Shag Rock 43, 62, 119
Shark, Blacktip 119
    Oceanic Whitetip 119
    Silky 120

Silvertip 120
Tawny Nurse 119
Thresher 120
Tiger 119
Whale 18, 22, 36, 120
Whitetip Reef 67, 119
Sharks 36, 51, 56, 57, 58, 64, 65, 70, 72, 78, 80, 118, 133, 151
Sharm el-Moiya 53
Sharm el-Sheikh 14, 15, 20, 31, 35, 43, 48, 53, 79
Shells 105
Shrimp, Banded Coral 113
    Basketstar 112
    Black Coral 110
    Clown Anemone 113
    Whip Coral 111
    White-banded Cleaner 112
    White-saddle Snapping 113
    Commensal 113
    Common Marble 112
    Crown-of-thorns 112
    Emperor 23
    Green-eyed Dancing 111
    Harlequin 111
    Henderson's Dancing 111
    Imperial 26, 28, 104, 112
    Pretty Snapping 113
    Red Spot Snapping 113
Shrimpfish 130
Shrimpgoby, Merten's 135
    Steinitz's 134
*Siderea griseai*129
Siderea thysoidea 129
Siganus luridus 146
Siganus rivulatus 146
Siganus stellatus 146
Sinai Peninsula 8, 18, 19, 31, 43, 59, 60
Siphonochalina siphonella 88
Siyul Kebira 64
Slug, Eyespot Wart 103
    Pustulose Wart 103
    Red Sea 104
    Varicose Wart 103
Snails 105
Snapper 66, 81, 83, 147
Snapper, Big Lip 147
    Black and White 81, 83, 147
    Dory 147
Sohal 148
Soldierfish, White-edged 147
Sole, Blackspotted 130
Solenostomus cyanopterus 25, 28, 131
Solenostomus paradoxus 25, 28, 130
Spanish Dancer 26, 27, 104, 112
Sphyraena barracuda 122
Sphyraena qenie 121
Spirobranchus giganteus 102
Spondylus marisrubri 105
Sponge, Colonial Tube 88
    Red Sea Red 88
Sponges 26, 88
Squid 77, 104, 105
Squid, Reef 77, 105
Squirrelfish 23, 147, 148

Squirrelfish, Bloodspot 147
Crown 148
Giant 148
White-tail 148
Starfish 26, 27, 29, 36, 97, 98, 99, 112
Starfish, Basket 26, 99, 112
Brittle 99
Coral Brittle 99
Crown-of-thorns 27, 29, 36, 98, 112
Klunzinger's Feather 98
Savigny's Feather 99
Sawtooth Feather 98
Stargazer 140
Stargazer, Dollfus' 140
Stenella longirostris 116
Stenopus hispidus 113
Stephanometra spp. 98
Stilbognathus longispinous 108
Stinging Alicia 97
Stingrays & electric rays 35
Stingray, Blue-spotted 118
Feathertail 118
St John's Island 72
Stonefish 35, 138, 139
Straits of Tiran 12, 20, 22, 43, 53, 54–57 80, 116
Subergorgia hicksoni 93
Sufflamen albicaudatus 152
Suez Canal 9, 11, 31, 61
Surgeonfish 148
Surgeonfish, Arabian 148
Sweeper, Dusky 150
Glassy 23, 35, 47, 53, 58,
Sweepers 23, 35, 47, 53, 58, 59, 62, 63, 64, 79, 138, 149, 150
Sweetlips 149
Sweetlips, Black-spotted 149
Striped 149
Synanceia verrucosa 139
Synodus dermatogenys 140
Synodus variegatus 140
Taba 15, 46, 47, 76, 132, 146
Table Corals, Acropora 95
Wide Acropora 94
Taeniura lymma 118
Talparia exusta 108
Talparia talpa 107
Tang, Sailfin 149
Yellowtail 149
Tangs 148
Tatralia cavimana 109
Terebra maculata 107
Terebra subulata 107
Tetrosomus gibbosus 146
Thalassia hemprichii 18
Thalassodendron ciliatum 18
Thalassoma klunzingeri 143
The Alternatives 60
The Gardens 51
The Tower 52

Thelenota ananas 100
Thor amboinensis 112
Tiaramedon spinosum 109
Tiran Island 18, 19, 20, 53, 117, 120
Toby, Dwarf 145
Topshell, Strawberry 106
Torpedo panthera 118
Toxopneustes pileolus 36
Trachyrhamphus longirostris 131
Trevally 150, 151
Trevally, Bigeye 150
Bluebar 150
Bluefin 151
Goldbody 150
Triaenodon obesus 119
Tridacna squamosa 105
Triggerfish 82, 152
Triggerfish, Blue 152
Bluethroat 152
Orange-striped 152
Picasso 152
Titan 82, 152
Yellowmargin 152
Tripneustes gratilla 99
Triton's Trumpet 28
Trunkfish 144, 146
Trunkfish, Thornback 146
Tubastrea aurea 94
Tubastrea micrantha 94
Tubipora musica 93
Turbinaria mesenterina 93
Tursiops truncatus 116
Turtle, Green 115
Hawksbill 115
Loggerhead 115
Turtles 22, 48, 66, 82, 115
Tylosorus choram 126
Umm Qamar Island 20, 64
Unicornfish 77, 148, 149
Unicornfish, Orangespine 149
Shortnose 149
Uranoscopus dollfusi 140
Urchin, Collector 99
Flower 36
Long-spined Sea 27, 100
Red Sea 36
Rock-boring 100
Rousseau's Coral 100
Slate Pencil 100
Toxic Leather Sea 99
Valenciennea puellaris 134
Vanderhorstia mertensi 135
Variola louti 136
Velvetfish, Crested 140
Vir philippinensis 113
Walkman, Red Sea 139
Whale, False Killer 117
Worm, Bispira Fan 101
Christmas Tree 102
Common Featherduster 101
Fan 101
Indian Feather Duster 101

Myzostomid 102
Peacock Bristle 102
Wrasse, Arabian Cleaner 143
Bird 143
Checkerboard 143
Chiseltooth 142
Common Cleaner 142
Klunzinger's 143
Napoleon 81, 142
Red-breasted Splendour 142
Red Sea Eightline 143
Ring 142
Rockmover 141
Vermiculate 142
Xenid, Pulsating 91
Zabargad 72
Zebrasoma desjardinii 149
Zebrasoma xanthurum 149